Back to Basics

How to make it through hard times

Written and illustrated by

Franz Sidney

Back to Basics

How to make it through hard times

Written and illustrated by

Franz Sidney

First Published in 2011 by Franz Sidney
Copyright © Franz Sidney
All rights reserved

ISBN 13: 9781466411524
ISBN-10: 146641152X

DEDICATION

This book is dedicated to all those who have helped me, by giving me their input and ideas, and to my husband and children for their support in this undertaking. But most of all, I dedicate my work to all those who are willing to work to bring a positive change into our society, through a return to traditional skills, hard work and traditional community values.

NOTES ABOUT THIS BOOK

This is an imperfect book, written by an imperfect human being, who is making an effort to help others, while using a foreign language. Please bear with me! Dealing with the software to get the layout just right was more difficult than writing the entire 160 pages.

I hope you will not dwell on the imperfections, but on the positive aspects. Each word comes straight from my heart and has been written with a smile on my face (especially when you see exclamation points!) Thanks for your patience!

ACKNOWLEDGMENTS

I would like to thank the happy bunch of proofreaders from all over this planet, who have devoted time and effort to review my book, and sort out all sorts of typos. I am also thankful to the many friends who kept asking me questions about gardening, food storage and health and encouraged me to put the answers together under one roof.

The Seven Blunders of the World
(Mahatma Gandhi)

Wealth without work

Pleasure without conscience

Knowledge without character

Commerce without morality

Science without humanity

Worship without sacrifice

Politics without principle

Rights without responsibilities

CONTENTS

INTRODUCTION

"If you don't like something change it; if you can't change it, change the way you think about it." (Mary Engelbreit)

I have been interested in self-reliance for almost 20 years and I have devoted a considerable time studying its principles and trying to implement them in my life. Although I am certainly not an authority on any subject I can honestly say that I have put to test many ideas and principles found in books, courses and websites and I am happy to share which ones have worked for me.

Many friends have come to me asking for explanations on all sorts of topics and this is my chance to put them all together under one roof. As many books or websites are either too technical and detailed, or just a compilation of lists of things to do, which leaves readers with no clue of *how* to get started, I thought I would fill the gap myself and save you browsing endless books and websites. I indeed took to my heart the well-known advice by novelist Toni Morrison:

"If there's a book you really want to read but it hasn't been written yet, then you must write it."

I have also added my personal opinion on why we are in such a mess (and not just financially speaking) and how we could possibly make the best of it, through hard work, a return to traditional values and thrifty living. You might agree or not with my ideas, and that's perfectly fine!

After all, as Oscar Wilde said, *"We are all in the gutter, but some of us are looking at the stars."* So, let's look at the stars and stop this unproductive moaning about the recession!

1
WHY WE ARE IN DEBT

"A wise and frugal government, which shall leave men free to regulate their own pursuits of industry and improvement, and shall not take from the mouth of labor the bread it has earned - this is the sum of good government." (Thomas Jefferson)

National and personal debt are pressing aspects of our present situation, together with unemployment, lack of economic growth, high taxation, impossible fuel prices and, of course, Robin Hood running our country into debt.

What? Did you say that the *Prime Minister* runs our country? You must be kidding. I tell you, it *must* be Robin Hood: he takes money from those who work hard, and gives it to those who don't want to work. A fair Minister would never do that, right?

After all, such a refined and educated person would surely apply those principles he learned from history and from past leaders when making decisions. If you are leading society, a government, a company or even a household, I invite you to review the timeless "Seven blunders of the world", which Mahatma Gandhi gave to his grandson Arun Gandhi, just before his death.

Just to mention a few blunders here, would we be in this situation if we could eliminate "wealth without work" and "rights without responsibilities"? I am sure that if you were discussing today's problems in the light of Gandhi's observations, there could be a great deal of conversation going on. Times have changed but timeless principles haven't. It is my view that as greed for power and money have replaced work, integrity and respect at all levels we have brought our country into this situation.

My beloved grandparents passed away some 8 years ago. Like many people of their generation they survived with dignity through the Great Depression and raised their kids with a small income, living in modest houses, having no car, TV or washing machine for years, and walking everywhere. They cooked from scratch, repaired things and made everything last for years. Even when they improved their financial situation they remained careful in their expenditures, thrifty and yet generous with others. They took time to help those in need and even saved some money that they left to their children when they passed away. They achieved their goal to have a united family. They were creative in using their small means to survive. Their enthusiasm and love for life was legendary despite their life-long poor health. I am sure that your grandparents were just the same. They were a great generation indeed. If my grandparents were able to return to life for a week and see the situation today I'm sure they would be laughing... or crying.

To have or to be?

"When prosperity comes, do not use all of it." (Confucius)

Our situation could be quite strange for an observer. We are all complaining about how expensive everything is, and yet the average household in Europe and North America boasts an abundance of cars, mobile phones, holidays, clothes, cable TV subscriptions and electronic gadgets, including large screen television sets and multiple computers - council estates included. Our salaries are not rising, and yet many eat out regularly, buy snacks and drinks during shopping trips, eat mostly ready meals, and spend weekends clubbing, partying, drinking or just spending as if there's no tomorrow.

Even our children are becoming obese and suffering from metabolic diseases, and yet we still drive everywhere. The school run is the time when those who could just walk to school in 25 minutes, drive to school, get stuck in the traffic for 24 minutes, and blame bike riders for slowing the traffic, but are always complaining that they are gaining weight.

But the weird thing is that our happiness doesn't seem to be proportional to the amount of goods we are piling in our closets. Quite the contrary.

We spend and spend, looking for that special thrill and excitement that is missing in our lives. We try new friends, new houses, new decorations, new diets, new cosmetics, schools and jobs, but sometimes there is a deep emptiness deep inside our souls.

What's going on? Why does the average person seem to be either in financial trouble or worried about it? Is there a big crisis coming

Yes, there are government mistakes, greedy bankers and mortgage lenders, rising prices, disasters, famines, and all the rest to make life more difficult. We can't stop tsunamis, crop failures, flooding, heat waves and fuel taxes. But we can learn a concept or two about money, marketing, shopping and debt and do more informed choices in the future. We can become self reliant, independent and skilled and help ourselves a great deal by being proactive and positive.

If it were possible, I would call self-reliance experts such as John Seymour (who, unluckily, has passed away) to run our nation. Instead, we have to endure listening to our Prime Minister labelling gardening as unskilled activity. Well, my dear PM, without skilled gardeners and farmers nobody would be able to eat! But every nation could do with cutting in half the amount of bureaucrats! What we really need to do is to learn to live within our means - and enjoy it.

The 'keep up with the Joneses' syndrome

"Too many people spend money they haven't earned, to buy things they don't want, to impress people they don't like."
(Will Smith)

We live in a media saturated world. We are bombarded every day by a tsunami of messages aimed to influence our opinions when it comes to spending. Soothing images stimulate our imagination and give us the illusion that all is well as long as we spend. Wherever we look, clever marketing messages fill up our mind with the concept of "buy now, pay later". We spend and over spend and we are not satisfied. We justify ourselves with the "great deal" we just couldn't miss, the zero interest offers and so on.

The hard truth is that when we "pay later", we are paying at least 10-20% more than our goods are worth, as either we are signing up for a loan through the shop or bank, or even when the offer states "interest free" it simply means that the amount we would have paid in interest is added to the initial price.

There is no such thing as "interest free" purchases as companies must pay high interest rates to the banks and must pay their invoices in full upon receipt of goods or within 3 months or so - certainly not after one year or every business would go bust. Retailers are not charities and their goal is not to help you "save more everyday" but to make you "spend more everyday" so that they can pay their costs and make a profit - or go bust.

Once we fix this concept in our mind, shopping becomes an entirely different experience. When we go shopping we can ask ourselves "What are these people trying to achieve with this offer?" and "What do I gain by buying or leaving this item and how is this item going to enrich my life?" In a way, we ought to become detectives.

The savvy consumer notices a lot of things. Advertising campaigns target our inner sense of self worth: we need to buy certain products in order to look as beautiful as the models in glossy magazines or we'll fail. As Thomas S. Monson declared in 2011, nowadays the trend seems to be "Spend it, wear it, flaunt it, because you are worth it."

We want to be like those apparently successful people who fill up the news headlines. We need to be ultra thin, super tanned, extra lean and forever young looking, with a perfect white smile; our skin has to be as smooth as a baby's skin even when we are 69. Wrinkles and "imperfections" are not acceptable in magazines, so we argue that they are not allowed in real life either, if we are to emulate our celebrities, our heroes.

However, if we were to see them after their Photoshopped photo-shoots, how many of these rich, famous or glamorous people have all the problems we have and even more? They are not immune from challenges even with their fantastic looks and large bank accounts. And spending lots of our money, time and energy to feel and look like celebrities in big, posh cars or houses shows just how much we feel we are worth.

Those who are running this rat race of keeping up with the Joneses would be better to stop quickly. Because sometimes that's all we are doing by buying the latest gizmos so we can be the first and feel special. Who on earth would spend his hard earned money for beautiful homes, accessories, trips, etc. if none of his acquaintances were there to cheer him up and compliment him?

Do we buy a fast car because we need to get to work on time or to impress others? Do we go to an event so we can tell everybody about it and show off our clothes?

A friend of mine worked for a nation-wide chain of shops selling computers and televisions. He related that when a new model of television would come out, the company would immediately display it in a prime position with an attached ridiculously high price.

Then those who were keen to show off their brilliant financial assets would walk in the shop and purchase the coveted object of desire. No doubt that soon after they were going to invite their friends via SMS or Facebook to admire their latest acquisition.

Only a couple of weeks later, the shop would then lower the price of this fantastic piece of technology to a more acceptable level and then more people would be interested in the "discount" and accept a "buy now pay later" deal. Shame that the same television was going to lose half of its value as soon as the latest model came out, although it hadn't lost even a pixel from its immaculate flat screen.

So, you tell me - who's smarter here? The marketing guy who is the brains behind this offer, or the guy who can't resist showing off his latest jewel to impress? Of course, shopping isn't the only victim of this race for the most impressive achievement. Even holidays, properties, fashion, kids' parties and other things follow this trend of showing off what we don't have or can't afford at all so we feel we are worth friends.

We even spend time checking the hundreds of friends (real ones or not?) we have on Facebook and getting worried if few of them write positive comments on our 'wall'. The truth is that for many people (not all, thankfully) shopping and spending money is a means to feel vibrant, powerful and alive, and the fact that they actually can't afford a certain way of life doesn't seem to bother them at all. They just buy everything on credit. They don't plan how they are going to cope in the future if they continue with their rate of overspending.

Well, that's exactly how entire nations have ended up on their knees, crushed by their debt (government debt and citizens' personal debt) and of course all the other problems. Perhaps it wouldn't look so glamorous if the things that we are still paying for had a red price tag attached, with a note of how much we owe to the bank. That would make a lot of our "friends" vanish very quickly.

But let's get back to the subject of retail stores offers. Because, my dear friends, I have the impression that the word "shopping" for some of us rhymes with "existing". And, that is a recipe for disaster and unhappiness.

2
LIVING A TRULY RICH LIFE

"Beware of little expenses; a small leak will sink a great ship."
(Benjamin Franklin)

To live an abundant life, we need to reverse the trend and go from "buy now, pay later" to "save now, buy later". This is achieved by committing to reject debt, unless it is absolutely necessary, for things such as a modest house or paying for further education. If we spend more than we earn, money controls us through the bondage of debt. If we spend less than we earn *we* control money; to achieve this we need to budget and to distinguish between wants and needs.

Now ask yourself: How many shoes are enough to make me happy? How many files do I need to download to feel content? How many drinks do I need to have to feel happy? How much make-up or fake tan do I need to slap on my face to feel I am presentable? Because the bottom line is that for some it's all about looking young, successful and rich or having it all now: house, car, furniture, holidays - that's why lots of us end up in debt. Add to this the current levels of unemployment and the general state of our health after decades of junk food and you can see why we need some serious change before our nation follows the destiny of Greece.

Unfortunately no material possession in this world can give lasting happiness after the initial thrill. No matter how many things one can buy, nobody can buy true friends or real health and happiness. Let's say it: you will *never* have enough of what you don't need. And what we need to survive is much less than what we actually buy.

The good news is that *the best things in life are free.* Good relationships, laughs, cuddles, spending time with our family, a walk in the nature in the fresh air - these are some of the things that build our lasting happiness whatever our financial situation. And they don't have to cost us a penny. As for the rest, well, I suggest we do one simple thing: plan ahead what you will need to spend.

Establishing a budget

"Thrift comes too late when you find it at the bottom of your purse." (Seneca)

So, you have decided to cut a little bit of your expenses, but they seem to be all equally necessary. Where do you start? Well, with budgeting of course. A budget is a list of all the expenses and revenues that we are planning to have. It is also a plan for saving, borrowing and spending. If the word budget sounds restrictive, call it "fund". Here is a simplified way to get started with a budget.

First, keep a record of your expenses and review where the money is going. Then, determine how you can reduce your expenses but cutting down on non-essential items. (Bills, mortgage etc. are to be paid first)

At this point you can establish a weekly or monthly family budget. Write down your average weekly/monthly earnings. Establish how much you need to pay to repay your debts and divide your expected expenditures in areas such as housing, food, bills, transportation, entertainment and so on. You can make your own worksheet or look for a free one on the internet.

Then discuss the budget with your family members and let them understand that they all need to contribute for the benefit of the family. Ask for enthusiastic contributions, don't just drop the budget on them before they understand the need of it or nobody will be motivated to keep it.

Keep track of your total debt versus earnings and decide how and when you are going to pay it off. You can also create a "Christmas fund", a "University fund" and so on.

Paying off credit card debt

"Credit buying is much like being drunk. The buzz happens immediately and gives you a lift... The hangover comes the day after." (Joyce Brothers)

Make a list of your debts and arrange them in order from smallest to largest. Now make a commitment to pay at least the minimum payment on all of them each month or a bit more to avoid years of debt.

Now pay off as much as you can on your smallest debt - you are trying to eliminate it. Every month include this repayment plan in your budget.

Once the smallest debt is paid off, use the same strategy on the next higher debt and so on. The more money you save, the more you can use to increase your monthly "paying off" standing orders. If you receive some unexpected money, resist the temptation to "treat yourself" with a shopping trip, and instead, pay off more debts. Not only you will be able to pay off all your debts but also you will gain a sense of achievement and increase your self-discipline. That alone is worth gold! (Well, almost!)

Eliminating credit cards and loyalty cards

"If you really desire something, but you don't need it at all, then you shouldn't buy it at all!" (Franz Sidney)

Personally, I feel that the only time that using a credit card is acceptable is when booking a trip abroad, as there are insurance benefits which as far as I know are not available for debit card or cash payers. However, I would prefer to pay for the trip's debt well before my departure! You might decide that it's time to eliminate some or all of your store credit cards. A wise decision indeed!

Did you know that store loyalty credit cards such as Debenhams, Next etc. are a clever way of putting more people in debt by making them work virtually for all their life as a customer to pay off the debt and the interest on their loan? And guess who benefits from your debt? The banks! Not you, for sure! But that's not how they advertise it to you. So, how does it work? Simple. When paying for your goods at the till, the shop assistant offers you an irresistible discount of around 10% on your items if you sign up to have a store card. You consider this a great opportunity for a nanosecond and give away your details and credit card number.

The smiling shop assistant enters your details in a dedicated machine, which immediately contacts a credit agency to check your credit rate. If it seems to be ok, you are then accepted within a minute.

But what you are actually doing is naively signing up a high interest open loan with a financial institution connected to the store. Yes, you might save £15 on a suit jacket, but when you start using the store card for your next purchase, unless you pay off your debt punctually, you will be actually paying more for your goods, on average 19.9% to 29.9%. This means that if you are late paying off your cards, you will be paying up to 30% more for your goods. And the credit company can easily raise interest rates at any time. Yes, they will send you a letter about it, but will you read a letter written so small that you need a magnifier? I guess you won't. The end point of using credit is that if a top would normally cost £30 you may pay £39 or more for it. A suit worth £85 would be £110.50 - who is getting the best deal?

The till operator earns a bonus from your signed financial agreement while you, the customer, are the real loser if you don't pay off your new debt in time. Figures may vary from retailer to retailer but the bottom line is that getting a store loan is not such a winning idea after all. Oh yes, some stores will say that you will be able to attend special evenings where special new stock will be shown just to you, the selected customer, and you might have a discount on the full price of the items. However, the same items will be on the shop displays within hours and further discounts will be offered anyway during the season, so having a store card is not the only way of receiving discounts.

With this in mind, heroically resist having any store credit card, and if you have one, consider paying off your debt as soon as possible and cancelling your account. You will save yourself a lot of future stress and anxiety. The same applies for buying items from retailers or catalogues which offer a "buy now pay later" formula that implies "buy now, pay *more* later".

As for using credit cards in stores, perhaps they are not as cool we are told. They just prove to the shop assistant and everybody else that we can't afford what we are buying, and therefore we are *living beyond our means*. How cool is that?

If you can't afford it you should *not* buy it, full stop. If you really want something, you can save for it every month (after paying off bills and credit cards) and then buy it. This is very important, because if you base your expenses on your impulse and mood instead of your essential needs, you will be buying things you don't really need at a higher price that you can't afford - how useful is this to erase your existing debt?

Remember: *you will never have enough of what you don't need.* You don't need to keep up with anybody else, either. Teach this concept to your children too. They can save towards something special instead of taking for granted that it will appear out of nowhere.

3
DON'T SHOP UNTIL YOU DROP

"The odds of going to the store for a loaf of bread and coming out with only a loaf of bread are three billion to one." (Erma Bombeck)

Have you ever said, "We're off to the supermarket for some bread and milk, dear"- just to return two hours later with several bags full of unplanned groceries and clothes? Then you are one of many people who cheerfully fall into the delightful trap set up by retailers. We all do that at least once a week. We try to focus on those two items we want and... Puff! our will power disappears as soon as we enter the store. Something magical seems to happen every time.

It can be difficult to resist those lovely clothes on sale, the new toy that your kids scream for, and the chocolate bars in the sweets department, and when you are near the tills and quite hungry there will be plenty of sugary treats to tempt your lot again before you start your journey home with an empty stomach and an even emptier bank account. So, just what went wrong there? Everything, dear. Everything. Let me show you how I become a supermarket fatality every time. Have you ever done any of the following?

- ✓ *Went out when you were rather hungry;*

- ✓ *Forgot at home your shopping list, reading glasses and pen;*

- ✓ *Went through all the aisles because you couldn't remember what you needed and then bought extra items but forgot the important ones;*

- ✓ *Stopped the children's screams by buying what they asked for;*

✓ Didn't compare prices, just picked whatever looked cheaper;

✓ Brought several credit and debit cards with you and had no idea of how much was left in your bank account.

I am sure that none of the above has *ever* happened in your family, correct? If this is the case, just move on to the next chapter and congratulate yourself for feeding a family of 4 with just £20 a week. For those who feel a bit differently, here's a suggested action plan. It works for me; it could work for you, perhaps tweaked to suit your personal shopping style. The important thing is to plan how you will deal with impulse shopping.

I have developed a little mantra before my shopping trips: if it's not essential food, clothing or cleaning stuff, I am not interested, thanks! Here are ten points to consider when planning to be parted from your money.

Step one: during the week go around the house and scribble a shopping list; don't just look at groceries, go check toiletries, broken items etc. and keep updating that list until the day you will actually go shopping.

Step two: look at your weekly budget (budget? What budget?) and work out how much you can safely spend that week - then reduce that amount by a few pounds.

Step three: before your shopping trip adventure starts, have a nice breakfast, snack or main meal containing carbs and proteins. Pasta, beans, or a bread roll with tuna will fill you up enough so that you won't crave food as much as on an empty stomach. An apple in the end will satisfy your desire for something sweet. Pop a fresh mint chewing gum in your mouth: it may prove helpful in defusing cravings for sweets.

Step four: if you have children, try to leave them at home with an adult! If they are coming with you, good luck! Make sure they have full stomachs and maybe "treat" them with a special chamomile tea or any relaxing herbal tea, just before leaving. If they are really tiny, prepare a couple of interesting toys that they can hold in their hands. Bring a bottle of cold milk ready to drink. It won't go off in an hour. If the kids are older, give them a copy of your shopping list each and a pencil so they can help you locate the items and they can tick one point per item. Each point can go to their special chart at home. They can also compare prices and make totals. Or they can play Sherlock Holmes and look for the hidden super-foods for you. Whatever works for your family will do, as long as you won't look like you are dragging several hungry and bored goats around the supermarket while customers stare at your failing attempts to put discipline them!

Step five: check that you have your debit cards or cash and your reading glasses/contacts/pencil/list. When is the last time you have checked your balance?

Step six: if you already know that you can't control yourself, go to the supermarket's ATM machine and withdraw just the amount you estimate you will need for the shopping before you enter the supermarket. Then hide the debit/credit card somewhere safe in your bag or car.

Step seven: go to the supermarket. Look at the time as you park. Give yourself 45-60 minutes maximum to finish your trip. Lots of customers say that when in supermarkets they tend to be a bit dazzled and blurred by the mix of colours. Walk by the tills and straight into the department that you need. *Compare prices!* Bring a calculator if needed. You can also use it to keep track of how much you are spending. Choose the cheapest item with the highest quality you can afford. I cannot stress enough how important it is to check the real price of the items we purchase.

Step eight: go to the till without passing through any aisle containing useless stuff, namely toys, gadgets or sweets. Choose a till without sweets on display!

Step nine: open your shopping bags and have the kids help you. Most stores will award you points for each bag. The points are equivalent to cash back which is a small bonus. Pay using your cash. If you have exceeded your budget, quickly see if you can eliminate something or use the debit card to pay for the excess.

Step ten: congratulate yourself and treat the kids with something special once home: a game together or a story. It doesn't have to be a physical treat. Record your expenditure in your family accountancy book.

So, summing up: plan ahead, go with a full stomach, buy what you need, ignore what's not in the list and use cash if you know yourself too well!

Alternative strategy: shop online. You will pay between £3.50 and £5 for delivery but there won't be clothes, electrical goods, or special offers and reduced items to tempt you. Possible benefits may include that you can see which offers are actually cheapest and you can see at all times how much the total will be, so you can cancel items when you have reached the amount you promised yourself not to exceed.

Let's assume that you spend a weekly £35 in your supermarket and 10% of it is saved because you followed the steps above. That's £3.50 saved per week. Multiply that by 52 weeks per year and you have saved £182! If your weekly expenditure is around £45, your savings can be a staggering £234 per year. That alone will pay for an average fully-comprehensive car insurance. Every little helps, they say in a nationwide supermarket. Yes, every little item adds up to the total you have to pay!

How to compare prices despite retail store attempts to confuse you

"If you can, you will quickly find that the greatest rate of return you will earn is on your own personal spending. Being a smart shopper is the first step to getting rich." (Mark Cuban)

Have you noticed a trick done by supermarkets, which can make you feel rather unsure of exactly how much you are spending or saving? It's evident especially when you look at the prices of fresh produce, bread and cereal bars.

Fruit and veggies

For example, you might be looking for apples and wonder which one will be the cheapest. You pick up a bag of 6 Granny Smiths and the price might be £1.45. You look at the label on the shelf and sure enough it says, "£1.45 per bag".

Then you look at Golden Delicious and the bag has 8 apples so you can't easily compare the price. You look at the shelf label and it's useless: "35p each". Uhm. Next, you look at a third type of apples and, sure enough, the price is specified per kg or per 100 grams. You have now collected three different types of pricing so you are unable to calculate quickly which option is the best for you.

This puzzling technique makes it virtually impossible for rushed customers to compare prices quickly while everybody else is trying to get to the same shelf or clamouring for the attention of their parent.

Cereal bars, crackers, biscuits, canned food and bread

The principle above applies to cereal bars: some are labelled with a price for a pack of 4, 5, 6 or 8, some with a price per bar, some per 100 grams or per kg. So you end up picking up some expensive cereal bars while thinking that you have saved money. Biscuits and crackers are also a little tricky to compare as they all differ in size, weight and packaging.

When you go to the sliced bread area it's even more confusing between large loaves, small loaves, half loaves, white, wholemeal and in-between. In the bakery area most breads don't even have all the ingredients listed so those who suffer from allergies and intolerances waste a lot of time trying to figure out what their food contains. Hello! Where's the labelling? Given that roughly 45% of customers will be long-sighted, and 99% will have left their reading glasses at home, how do retail stores expect them to read labels written in a size 8 font? Amazing. Every little helps, right? So, give us clear labelling and clear prices or customers will look elsewhere!

The maths behind this entire muddle

So, how do you deal with this muddled information? Because it can be annoying to spend more money, just because prices are made to be difficult to interpret. There are at least two options. One is to refresh your mental maths skills. The other is to bring pen, paper and a calculator, stand there and work out what is the real price of things. Now I am not saying that your 'A' level in maths is not good anymore, but one thing is to study to pass a test, and another is to apply what you learned in real life. In fact, in theory any 10 year old should be able to help you compare prices expressed in multiple measuring units. However, it has been stated in many recent news articles that UK companies often need to retrain their youngest employees to teach them the basics of maths so they can cope with everyday problems. Here's your golden opportunity to refresh the entire family's math skills!

Supermarket maths (supermaths!)

Just in case you have no clue, let's look at an example. A bag of Braeburn apples is on sale for £1.85. There are six apples in the bag. So if we divide £1.85 by 6 we see that we are paying about 30 pence for each apple.

A bag of "Fun Size" apples may be on sale for £1.24 and there are 8 apples. So the individual price is 15 pence each. These are cheaper apples... but smaller. You will need a price per weight to work out exactly what you are paying for your apples!

Once you have done this exercise at home a few times you will become faster and faster and soon you will memorise the prices of each item and the way of getting to that final price. A productive activity to try is to do all these calculations with your kids to help them with their maths skills. If they are far too good at maths and laugh at such a ridiculously easy task, ask them to do the same operation in a foreign language or calculate the price of an entire meal! That should give them some reassurance that there is still much to learn in life and Mum (or Dad) is ahead of the game. Aren't they?

Size ain't everything

Sometimes the packaging of a product makes us think that we are getting much more than we actually are. While products such as spaghetti are tightly packaged, others are placed in much bigger boxes than necessary, from Easter eggs to breakfast cereals to fancy gift packages with crayons and stationery.

If you don't believe me, when you are home pick up an average big box of cornflakes. Note in your mind the weight of the product, 500g. Now open the box, pick up the bag with the cereals and open it. Carefully remove the air and rearrange the cornflakes so they fit in a tighter space. Cut off or roll the excess plastic. Now cut the cereal box so that it will fit just an inch over the cornflakes bag.

You will see that the product fills only 1/3 of the box and therefore a box that is 2/3 smaller could easily accommodate your cereals. So why don't cereals come in smaller boxes? Smart question! If you show anybody that tiny box of cereals and attach the normal price to it, for example £1, that person will complain that the cereals are very dear.

We naturally look for the lowest price and the biggest box. However, the outer box is not a final representation of the size of the contents and as long as we identify the product value by packaging and size we are not likely to save any money. So, next time you buy your breakfast cereals, you may want to look instead at the price per 100 grams or kg. and compare those. Supermarkets are losing money by using bigger boxes as they occupy more space in trucks, they use more fuel, they do more work to move them around and occupy more space on the shelf.

Why do they waste so much money for bigger packaging? Because it is worth it. You, the customer, are looking for something *big* to perceive you are getting value for money. Meanwhile, prices of grains and cereals have skyrocketed worldwide and the hike is cleverly disguised by keeping the price on the box stable and shrinking the inner contents box while the outside box gives you the false idea that you are getting a good deal.

How we regularly ruin our finances when shopping in town

"Fate often puts all the material for happiness and prosperity into a man's hands just to see how miserable he can make himself with them." (Don Marquis)

Going to the town or city centre can be quite exciting (for the children), tiring (for the lady in the family) and boring (for the man in the family). At some point somebody will be dirty, tired, hungry or thirsty or all four, usually within an hour. Sometimes, after the temporary buzz of buying several items, we feel quite miserable, too. A quick shopping trip may spell problems if we are already in debt. However, we can improve the outcome by planning ahead what we want to achieve. This will also eliminate our sense of guilt, as we shall avoid over spending.

Prepare a shopping list and decide which shops you will visit. Bring some light snacks, some wipes if you have toddlers or babies and a small bottle of water (any drink containing sugar will inevitably make you thirstier so you will spend more money).

Remember that if you give sweet foods you are more likely to deal with thirsty *and* super energetic children. Use cash only if you can or hide just one debit card perhaps in the bottom of your bag, so you won't use it unless it is an emergency. Leave *all* your credit cards at home! Remember your target is to eliminate debt, not to increase it.

If you are trying to save money, try to avoid takeaways and sandwich shops: for the price of a single sandwich (minimum £2-£3) you can buy a whole loaf of bread and plenty of fillers. So a family of four can easily save around £10-£12 just by not eating outside. If you go shopping in town once a week for a year, you can spend or save over £500 - you decide where the money is staying, your account or somebody else's!

Compare prices using your calculator or your super-maths mind. Then, if you feel the urge to purchase a particular item that is not essential, leave it to the end of the trip. By then you may find that your mind is off it and you won't feel like buying it anymore.

When you arrive home, calculate how much you spent and if you have spent less than expected, allocate the amount saved to pay off some more of your debt or put it in a savings account. As they say, "Every little helps". If you are well off and you find saving accounts not worth the hassle, buy silver coins instead! At least they will retain a good value over the years, unlike any currency around.

4
HOW TO SAVE MONEY ON MOST THINGS

"I have learnt to seek my happiness in limiting my desires, rather than attempting to satisfy them." (John Stuart Mill)

Here is a little list that I have put together after browsing books and websites and discarding any impossible, weird or inappropriate advice. Hopefully you will be able to pick a few that you feel you can cope with. Enjoy!

- ✓ Use only one car per household

- ✓ Have a mobile only if essential

- ✓ No mobile phones for children; yes to teen-agers *if* they pay for them

- ✓ Don't eat out often (if in huge debt, never eat out!)

- ✓ Cook from scratch and make your own bread

- ✓ Shop as little as possible and when appropriate, choose the store brand or sale items that are really convenient

- ✓ Drink water instead of alcohol, juices and other chemical-laden stuff

- ✓ Do without call waiting and other additions to your home phone contract

- ✓ Say bye-bye to cable/satellite TV!

- ✓ Grow your own food and then eat that!

- ✓ Buy fewer clothes, accept hand-me-downs, learn how to sew, repair and renovate clothes, participate in clothes swapping parties

✓ Don't heat up the whole house to 20°C (68°F) in winter! Turn down the thermostat and use jumpers, socks, cardigans and blankets.

✓ If there is a sale of food, use it to stock up your pantry - prices are on the rise.

✓ Remember that the least expensive filling foods are beans, potatoes, rice and soups - and potatoes are the easiest crop to grow!

✓ Unplug or turn off any electrical appliance that is not in use

✓ Don't buy a new pet once yours has gone - pets can cost a fortune!

✓ Have 5 minute long showers every other day, not a bath every day

✓ Avoid electronic gadgets and toys

✓ Do only 30°C (86°F) washes in your washing machine, wash by hand small items, clean stains before putting garments in the washing machine.

✓ Learn how to repair things: shoes, furniture, doors, plumbing, and painting.

✓ Replace expensive cleaning products, shampoos and cosmetics with traditional home made ones.

✓ Use Freegle to find free items. The link is: http://ilovefreegle.org/about
Freegle is an email list hosted on "Yahoo! Groups", that allows you to give stuff away when you need to get rid of it but don't want to throw it in the bin. Use cheapcycle too, to buy or sell for cheaper used goods.

✓ If possible, don't do any business with anybody whose only phone number starts with 0808, 0842, 0843, 0844,

0845, 0870, 0871, 0872 and 0873! Lots of catalogues, banks, insurance companies and other businesses charge customers a rate per minute (for example 10p per minute) and it all adds up. This practice should be made illegal in my opinion - however, meanwhile for UK numbers we can go to a useful website called SayNoTo0870. Once there, write in the search box the expensive phone number you are to call and you will find the cheaper alternative listed.

✓ Be aware when switching electricity, gas or telephone provider. Resist hard door sales and do your research before switching. Many times the offer that sounds so temping only lasts for the initial period and then the price increases again. I was once offered some good discounts for using a new electricity provider; the seller stated in good faith that most shops I used would have been offering me discounts because of my new provider giving me vouchers. I declined his offer and called the company directly, but after talking to three or four different operators it became clear that none of them was able to indicate exactly how I was going to get such discounts and to what companies and percentages they applied, and their website didn't give any clue either. There are UK comparison websites such as USwitch and Moneysupermarket.com (and many others), but be aware that some of these sites get commission for selling a particular brand or offer, so search around carefully.

✓ *If you don't need it or can't afford it, even a good deal is bad for you!*

Getting together with like-minded people

It is my personal view that a big crisis is coming and when that happens we shall be better off if we are cooperating with like-minded people. We need to become self-reliant, learn more traditional skills and share them with others, by teaching, by learning, and by bartering. Buy a property with some land if you can - more land is a better investment than more rooms to heat!

Do read self reliance books such as the one from John Seymour mentioned in my links at the end of this book; learn why we need to return to producing our own wealth instead of buying or importing goods: until the 60s, skills like shoe-making, spinning, sewing, baking, growing crops, raising animals, and so on were found in every village and people never needed to travel hundreds of miles to find a skilled craftsman. Communities were close-knit and self-reliant. Now we all want white-collar jobs or singing, dancing and drama jobs, and when we can't find exactly what we want, lots of us just go on 'job-seekers allowance' and refuse to work with our hands. Then we complain that there is no work - so how come that most of our fruit pickers are not British? And lots of our factory workers? So, there *is* work, but of course, nobody wants to make his hands dirty! Oh, well - then we could change our attitude!

Well - you might say - but factory workers and fruit pickers are not well paid at all. I am very aware of that. But guess why they can't pay too much? Because big supermarkets force them to keep their prices low, or lose orders. And why does this happen?

Because we demand low-priced food and clothes, and expect to pay £2 for a chicken or a fiver for a pair of jeans. How do you think it's possible to pay for the vet bills, the food, the slaughtering, the processing, packaging and lorry costs, plus fuel, and still make *any* profit from £2? This game can't go on much longer.

We need to pay what food is worth if we want to support our own farmers in this crisis. Ten years ago there were around 30,000 dairy farms in the UK. Now, every day across Britain one of our 11,000 remaining dairy farmers is turning their back on dairy farming and selling off their herds. Our dairy industry is in desperate need of an economic turnaround. Some skills are disappearing completely - wake up!

5
TRAVELLING CHEAPLY FOR WORK AND LEISURE

"A penny saved is a penny earned." (Benjamin Franklin)

I won't give you any advice on which countries are cheaper as everything is fluctuating and you can find better information on specialised sites on the internet. However, my main point is, what do you define as a holiday? A break from what you usually do and see, perhaps on a beach, in a sunnier country? Or long walks around archaeological sites, ruins or famous museums?

Whatever your reasons, research well before departing from your hard-earned money. And if you can't afford a holiday, perhaps you can afford a house swap for a week with a friend who lives somewhere different.

For example, your area might offer good shopping facilities and children's entertainment while your friend's area might have a forest, lakes or some yoga courses. It's worth researching what is available and then you can propose the swap. This way you will only spend money to get to and from your destination, and of course you will take care of the other property as if it were your own or even better. The most important thing is of course to avoid going abroad to spend money if you have a lot of debt and are worried about paying your bills. If you can afford a holiday, there are plenty of little tricks that can help you to save money once you arrive at your destination.

One of the biggest expenses on holiday is having all your meals out. Research beforehand what is available in the area you are visiting in terms of local shops and supermarkets. You might find that within 10 minutes travel from the tourist area there is a supermarket where you can buy everyday staples cheaply that won't break the bank. Eating in any town centre - especially in a tourist area - will always give a blow to your finances and sometimes the price of food reflects the value of the location and not the quality or quantity of the ingredients.

One such example is when we went on holiday to Tuscany in Italy and ventured into the fine city of Florence. An average ice cream then cost around £1.50 - £2 in any bar, but when we reached the town centre near Galleria degli Uffizi, the price suddenly jumped to £7! It must have been a gold ice cream, of course!

A very good alternative to staying in Hotels and B&B is agritourism, which is staying at a traditional farm house where lots of the food served comes from the farm itself and is therefore genuine and - at times - cheaper. Entertainment can range from horse riding to free walks in the countryside, petting animals or going to a local beach or festival.

If you are interested in Museums, research prices online and see if you can purchase a ticket in advance to avoid queues and stress. However, bear in mind that some websites will charge you a £10-15 one off fee for reserving such tickets online!

Look also for holiday bartering websites. I found one in Italy where people from all walks of life were offering free holidays to anyone who would for example paint their home for free, or fix a broken pipe, teach them some English and so on. The possibilities are endless and with cheap flights it is still possible to spend some quality time abroad and perhaps learn or share a skill.

If you are off to a traditional Mediterranean beach holiday, check beforehand how the beaches you will visit are manned and managed. If you go to a free beach the policy is "first come first served" and by arriving by 8am. you will secure a nice space for your towel near the water. The tide is much shorter in Mediterranean countries so you don't have to move backwards every hour!

A free beach is exactly what it is called - free, and you might find difficulties finding services, disabled toilets, or in fact any toilets or showers. You might have to walk on dunes and leave your car 1 mile away from the beach. But they are usually so beautiful that it's worth all your efforts. Bring your packed lunch and a cool bag for some water and you can spend a day relaxing with your travel companions, almost for free.

If you choose a managed beach, things are different. A company will be in charge and you will be charged for parking, services, getting a seat and umbrella, and so on. You will be assigned your seat and you might find the place impossibly crowded with the inability to gain any space within your row of chairs. However some beaches will offer gym, dance, and fitness sessions, and even massage depending on how much you wish to spend.

If you decided that after all you are not going abroad, camping is also a good way of having a local holiday and sustain the economy of your own country. You can buy or rent most equipment and ask experienced campers about the best sites and facilities before committing.

Whatever holiday you are choosing, establish in advance how much you think it will cost, and then add around 30% for food, drinks and extras. Then save every month a good amount of money towards that holiday, after paying off credit cards minimum payments, loan repayments, bills etc. It might take you two or more years to save enough money - you will appreciate your holiday even more if you have worked hard for it. Pay everything with a debit card or cash before departing, and bring enough money to cover for the local expenses, but try not to spend it all - you don't have to!

6
SURVIVING THE BIG CHRISTMAS MADNESS

"Once again, we come to the Holiday Season, a deeply religious time that each of us observes, in his own way, by going to the mall of his choice." (Dave Barry)

I love this quote "Oh, for the good old days when people would stop Christmas shopping when they ran out of money". Most people enjoy the Christmas season but I must admit that in recent times, I have started to feel stressed about all the pressure to buy, consume and have non-stop parties. What a silly way of remembering the One whose birth we celebrate. We have gone from exchanging simple gifts and visits with our loved ones to a huge shopping madness and a series of activities, parties and celebrations that are completely disconnected from the reason for the season.

What shops help you to do for Christmas is not to "save more every day" but "spend more every day" for items you don't need at all. Christmas offers start as early as September 8th and don't always include any fantastically good deal or any useful, lasting goods. We might spend precious hours signing hundreds of Christmas cards with pre-printed messages but we often fail to talk to our dear friends to wish them Merry Christmas and actually ask how they are doing. Christmas is treated very superficially by many and can be a tiring, stressful or expensive event for many people. Most of all, Christmas is becoming simply unaffordable to those who feel the pressure to spend as if their life depends on it. Let's see in ten sections what we can do to defend ourselves from this tsunami of tinsel wrapped paraphernalia. We ought to remember what Christmas is really about as I think that we have lost track of its meaning with all this mad Christmas shopping followed by the madness of after-Christmas sales. Just what happened to the season when people felt like they wanted to help others and be good? Peg Bracken once said, *"Gifts of time and love are surely the basic ingredients of a truly merry Christmas"*. She has made a very good point indeed, don't you think?

Planning ahead

One. Buy, or even better, *make* only gifts that are needed or welcomed by the recipient. For example, if your daughter has been nagging you about a new jumper since October you can buy her one for Christmas. Yes, she *can* wait two months - I promise. And, who said that you have to buy more than one expensive gift for each person? If she wants it sooner, she can earn it by working around the house or doing baby sitting, washing the car etc.

Two. Cheap Christmas shopping starts after the 2nd of January or a bit earlier. Avoid the mad crowds, bad weather, queues, silly prices and impulsive buying and shop when things are calm (don't shop in December in this case!) Sales often happen also after January 10th. In fact, shops can be almost empty between mid January and Easter while customers recover from their spending sprees. And when they are dying for a customer, you might get a good deal. Haggling still exists, especially at local markets and independent shops, but also in chain shops if you have cash ready. Buy what you really meant to buy, wrap it beautifully (maybe with fabric!), and tick it off the list of next year and rest in peace. Pick up old Christmas cards, cut off the best illustrations and put them in a craft box. Later on they will be useful to decorate objects with decoupage or to create collage or new cards.

Three. In December you will be facing higher heating and food bills, and paying for trips to concerts and parties, and lots of extra money just goes into last minute problems. To avoid being stressed out, save for example ten pounds a month starting from January, and put it away just for Christmas expenses. That will work out cheaper than buying with credit cards and increasing your debt.

Four. When organising your Christmas meals and parties, try to propose a potluck buffet type meal. Everybody brings something and shares it, and you all save some time, money and hassle.

Five. If step four didn't work (lazy friends, huh?) try to eat at home instead of going out for a meal. Design your menu keeping in mind budget, taste, your waistline and health. You don't *have to* become bloated, drunk and sleepy after a huge Christmas meal. A good idea is to prepare some food in advance and freeze it.

Six. Contrary to what magazines tell you, you don't need to buy new outfits for the Christmas season or special occasions, holidays etc. Have a look in your wardrobe and find new accessories to revamp your vintage clothes. A well fitting little black or red dress can be the base for any smart combination. Men always look good with dark trousers and a good quality shirt. If you can sew, add a festive trim to a plain outfit or add some beads on the neckline of a sober top. Creativity wins. Even a simple large t-shirt can be transformed into a skirt in less than a minute. Just for fun, look at the instructions and drawings here: http://www.cutecircuit.com/30secondskirt

Remember that sometimes less is more. In this case, the less debt, the more peace of mind. Would you rather have a wardrobe full of clothes or a bank account full of savings?

Seven. You don't need to buy new Christmas decorations every year. They probably come mostly from China and all your neighbours will have an exact copy in their home. How boring! Instead, you can create your own decorations using local materials and your creativity. You can design and decorate a nativity set and anything to hang on your tree by using art and craft packs, sewing, beading, papier-mâché, stained glass, glitter, dried fruit or just your imagination, and the help of your friends, children or grandchildren. Chances are that you will do such a good job in making your own decorations, that you will treasure them for years, especially the imperfect ones - because making things with your hands is always special. There are plenty of ideas on how to make your own decorations in library books and on the internet. Children love making decorations - again, there is no need to buy those expensive sets from supermarkets - you can re-use what you have.

Eight. December is usually the time when people mix more with others and get more colds and flu then ever. You won't fancy a trip to the chemist if you are feeling under the weather and it's frustrating to drive or park anywhere on icy roads. Be prepared and stock up in advance with home remedies for winter ailments (from herbal teas to essential oils, your usual medications and some good old honey).

Nine. Christmas parties won't be overly expensive if you add several fun games that everybody will enjoy (white elephant for example), or get some good music to listen to, rent a couple of fun videos, or even get ready for carol singing. Overall remember that Christmas can be a special time for your family and friends to be together and enjoy the company of each other. I can't remember what I received or what I've eaten but the memories of my children cuddling up with me are priceless. People are more important than things.

Ten. Some good stocking fillers are in the children's gift area. Check them out! You are worth it! Also, check out your dollar stores in the U.S. or Poundland in the UK for cheap stocking fillers. Throughout the next chapters I will show you how to make special gifts for everyone without breaking the bank. I'd love to hear what you have made for your loved ones! As this book is in black and white I didn't add some colourful projects to inspire you. I thought it was better to keep the price down, as I am trying to make you save money! However, there will be plenty of opportunities in the future, starting with my blog.

7
THE ART OF DE-CLUTTERING

"Enjoy the little things, for one day you may look back and realize they were the big things." (Robert Brault)

A gift is something we donate to others to make them feel special. It can be an item, an action, your time or work, or something you make. Spending less on gifts doesn't necessarily mean that the gift won't be appreciated. If the receiving end is expecting something expensive from you, then it's a good idea to lower his or her expectations to a reasonable and affordable amount of money. Gifts don't necessarily need to be bought in a shop by the donor. By the way, somebody's clutter may be somebody else's treasure.

Identifying "clutter" and getting rid of it for good is a good way to find our hidden treasures just in time for Christmas. Living surrounded by clutter is a choice that some people make by not getting rid of it regularly. For some, it is perfectly fine to step on piles of dirty laundry, old bills and empty crisp bags while walking from A to B. For others it may be quite distressing, as they can't think clearly while their multitasking mind is picking up lots of visual messages while also trying to focus on a different task.

If you want to get rid of debt and save money, it really helps to have a clear mind, develop stronger organisational skills and be able to find your bills immediately so you can pay them before charges apply. De-cluttering the family home is for some people quite a powerful, liberating experience that brings a more focused mind. Why not have a try?

It's good to work on de-cluttering for at least ten minutes every single day, perhaps with the sound of some cheerful or relaxing music. With determination, you will get to the bottom of the pile and even discover some hidden treasures while you go.

You can de-clutter as a team, too. Involve your children; put a timer and whoever sorts out the highest number of items gets a treat. They might want to play that game every day, you never know! I love de-cluttering while listening to inspiring music. Have you tried doing it while playing Gustavo Dudamel at the Proms - Arturo Márquez Danzon No. 2 on YouTube? This is music that will rock you! And now, let's look for your hidden treasures!

The first thing you can do is to have a good look around your house and put away anything that has been sitting there for a long while, doing absolutely nothing to enrich your life and make you feel happy or fulfilled. No, I don't mean husbands, wives, partners or children, you cheeky!

I mean those tacky ornaments that Aunt Ruby brought you from a popular seaside resort 20 years ago, those champagne glasses that you have never dared to use in case they broke, the impossibly tight shoes that you stopped using after the first day, the World Encyclopaedia bought in the 80s or your collection of picture frames, dolls, cards, empty cans, broken necklaces, old mobile phones, ancient PCs and whatever else we tend to fill our house with. In other words, clutter. Because if something is not used at all or doesn't quite decorate either, to you it's just clutter. But to somebody else it may be a very welcome gift.

How to sort out pre-loved items

De-cluttering your house might help to give gifts to lots of people without spending a penny, and in any case your house will instantly look roomier and tidier without having to move to a bigger property. Remember, you control things, not the other way around. Why do we let "things" use all our space and make us feel crammed, oppressed, stressed out and depressed? And why do we spend money on "things" that we don't need at all and won't make us happy 24 hours later? We can avoid a lot of financial problems by stopping impulse buying and hoarding. We can avoid much of the clutter by dealing with mail, homework, packaging and documents promptly. And now, let's get into it. Deeply.

Depending on the amount of clutter gracing your property you might need to work room by room every day for an hour. Simply pick up 3 large bags or carton boxes and scribble on them respectively: bin, charity shop, possible gift.

In the first container you will put anything that can't possibly be reused, donated or recycled. When you finish with that, immediately proceed to empty that container in your bin and forget about it. This can be such a liberating experience!

In the second container for the charity shop, you can put all the items that would be wasted if thrown away but couldn't possibly be appreciated as a gift by your loved ones. When the container has all those objects from around the house, promptly walk to the car, open the boot and put it there. Then go to your calendar and write down in which day of that week you will arrange a trip to your local charity shop. If the goods are bulky, some charity shops arrange picking them up. Phone in advance. Many shops cannot accept anything operated by electricity.

Finally, the last container will be filled with those objects which you hope will make somebody happy. Go through each item and ask yourself which relative, neighbour or friend could make use of it. If it's still looking as good as new, by all means wrap it up nicely and offer it at the next occasion, be it birthday or Christmas. Congratulate yourself! You have saved some money and made somebody happy. Or you might sell your item on eBay or on Cheapcycle if it's quite interesting, or in a car boot sale for one or two pounds.

Think laterally and creatively. Strong metal containers can be used as ashtrays or to put paint or candles. Old bank statements and letters usually have a third of a page or a full page that is completely white; cut it off, put the statement in the paper bin (or shred it if you prefer) and keep the strip of paper in a stack ready for your next shopping list or "to do" list.

Old shoes and bags might have interesting buckles, ornaments or shoelaces/strings, which can be put into a craft box for later use. Some old clothes and hats may be useful if your kids like dressing up as adults to have fun. If the fabric is still good, cut it off and use it to make pet clothes, drawstring bags, shopping bags and so on.

Broken paste jewels may be repaired or donated to somebody who loves making beaded necklaces and decorations; or it can be placed in your craft box to decorate your next gift.

Old curtains with a nice pattern can be cut up to make stylish shopping bags, or use net curtains as tree or plant netting to protect fruit from birds. Any fabric from any clothes, as long as it is not torn, can be used for quilting projects. Old knitting wool can be used in strands to repair holes in thick socks or to teach the first steps of sewing to a child. Large containers or baskets can be decorated to be able to hold plants, towels, firewood and other items in style. Old fabric from bed covers can also be recycled to make cleaning rags, or if pretty enough, to make toy bags. Fabric of any type can be used to make unique rugs for your home.

You can also join the local Yahoo groups Freecycle (now Freegle) and Cheapcycle to give away or sell your items. Don't expect to become rich! Once you have emptied your house (and loft or shed) from lots of useless stuff, and perhaps made some cash on eBay by selling some pricey items, you may look differently at acquiring more useless stuff in the future. In my house I have a policy of "no ornaments please" as they are taken to the charity shop within 24 hours or given away to others if I feel they are pretty enough to adorn their shelves - not mine, thank you. My idea is that no matter how many thing I buy, my little property isn't going to expand to accommodate them and I will feel tighter every day, thereby making it stressful to enjoy my space (or lack of it!).

8
HOW TO MAKE YOUR CHILDREN EARN THEIR GIFTS

"If you want your children to turn out well, spend twice as much time with them, and half as much money." (Abigail Van Buren)

Although I am not an expert in child behaviour, I have found some interesting ideas to save some money on children's gifts while convincing them to help at home. Yes. It can be done! Gifts for kids can be a touchy subject. If your children/grandchildren have grown up taking for granted that they will receive lots of expensive toys and electronic gadgets, and they start to resemble the Dursleys in the Harry Potter books, what can you do when times are hard and your budget cannot stretch?

Well, you do what the Government does: cut the funding and raise the tax or your expectations. Gifts come once or twice a year, are few, of good quality and reflect the family budget and the child's attitude. If in doubt regarding cutting on gifts, please read Unicef's report on children's happiness.

It states that the UK sits at no. 27 in the list of happy countries examined in the study. The report basically says that children in the UK are the unhappiest because their parents spend money on them instead of spending time with them.

Children want time, not stuff, states the report, and instead we work all hours to raise our income and buy them *things,* we drop our children at the nursery from the age of 6 months so we can return to work as soon as possible and then we complain about our spoiled and bored children.

So why did we bother having children if we didn't want to spend time with them? Why do we buy stuff to compensate for the time we should spend enjoying our children? Unicef report: (http://www.unicef-irc.org/publications/pdf/rc7_eng.pdf)

Perhaps it's time to stop putting mothers under pressure to work at all costs, because once you've paid the child-minder, if you have an average salary there won't be much left in your account. But let's return to your children and how they will cope without a mountain of "stuff" at Christmas and festivities. Can they cope? Oh, yes, they can and they may be pleasantly surprised by their coping skills.

So, one day you sit down calmly and explain to your family that you are not the Bank of England (thank God!) and money doesn't grow on trees, as they might have believed up to now. Starting today, you will state firmly that each child will receive a maximum of one or two gifts for Christmas from you and there will be a limit to the total amount spent. Such limit will *not* exceed your budget.

While your stunned offspring are still trying to make sense of what's going on, you kindly add that of course they can still get the iPhone they wanted or their favourite Lego set - as long as they *earn* them. Now graciously close the wide open mouths of your children and escort them into the kitchen to look at the newly prepared reward chart enhanced with a shiny tasks list; have them sit at the table with you "for a nice little chat about helping in the house and working as a team".

With a maternal smile painted on your face, (even if you are the father) show to your kids the tasks that Mum and Dad perform daily for the benefit of the entire family, from emptying the bin to washing the dishes, making beds, washing the cars, folding the laundry and so on. Of course, you have prepared that list beforehand and worked out how the system works by asking all your friends how they did it, or by browsing the internet forums for hints. You might have a chart with plus and minus points, each equivalent to ten pence - it's up to you. You will list on one side the tasks that from now on your children will be supposed to get on with as "members of our great team, the

Jones family", you will say proudly. On the other side of the list there will be some extra jobs listed in which they can earn real money. Make sure you list very easy jobs, too, in order to include everyone from 3 year old onwards. Rotate the tasks weekly to avoid boredom and to be fair to all.

Now, before your children fully realise what they are getting into, with your sweetest tone of voice ask, "Who would like to help me with the dishes this week? If you don't volunteer I can pick who I want and you might end up with the jobs you like the least." Ask your youngest kids simple things such as "Can you help Mummy to set up the table? Can you help to empty the washing machine or fold the socks? Can you put away your toys?"

Hopefully you will get few complaints and resistance but in the end your children will accept responsibilities. They can start with little things such as setting the table; when the tasks are done naturally and regularly by them you can add some more, simple tasks and then praise your kids regularly as they grow up into independent adults who know how to work and solve problems.

Children love to be appreciated, praised and made to feel useful, especially if they have been taught to help since they were young. However, don't despair if they are already teenagers and don't help at all yet. It is still possible to refresh their minds on who is in charge in the house. If they disagree with that, a look at the rent book, or council tax bill will prove otherwise.

Spend some time organising which task is to be done by whom on that week. When the tasks for the day are done, simply draw a tick, a star or place a sticker on the chart. By the end of the week, the children should have achieved a number of points which you can translate into a special time with you, a trip to the park, doing crafts together, a bonus towards a Christmas gift or whichever free activity you think your child will look forward to and you can cope with. Each family is different and you need to work out what will motivate your own children.

If the children start crying, throwing tantrums or whatever, simply state gently and firmly, "These are the new rules, I expect you to keep them" and walk away. The tantrum will eventually stop if you are not there. (No audience, no performance!) Then, expect things to get started. Phyllis Diller once said that *"Most children threaten at times to run away from home. This is the only thing that keeps some parents going."* Cheer up! Things will work out. After all, you are in charge.

If jobs don't get done, ask the child who is in charge of each task, to get started and stay there, until he is getting on with his task, then praise him for doing so. Once the children see that you mean business they will get on with their house chores, eventually accepting that at home people help one another and mother is not their servant but their delightful duty manager.

Once each child is helping at meal times, tidying up his room and helping with laundry, you should have some free time which you can spend however you wish to. Your children will learn those precious home-making skills that seem to be lacking in these new times of high-tech entertainment and takeaways munched in front of the TV. Of course things won't be perfect. Someone said that cleaning up with children around is like shovelling during a blizzard. We understand that when children try to help they might cause more mess than they clear. However, I think it's worth giving them a chance to learn.

If you have any problems in getting things done do look on the internet for specific coping strategies - this book is not meant to cover all subjects in depth but simply to give you a head start. A good start could be looking at this link:

www.more4kids.info/549/best-parenting-websites

May I also suggest a splendid book on the subject, *"The entitlement trap - How to Rescue Your Child with a New Family System of Choosing, Earning, and Ownership"* by Richard Eyre. This is a good guide to learn how to instill children with a sense of ownership, responsibility, and self-sufficiency. At the heart of their plan is the "Family Economy" complete with a family bank, chequebooks for kids, and a system of initiative-building responsibilities that teaches kids to earn money for the things they want.

I suggest this author or anybody with a similar approach, as I believe that responsible children are more likely to appreciate that in difficult times a mountain of gifts is just not going to happen.

Some cheap and easy stocking fillers

Not everybody likes to fill up those hungry-looking stockings with candies and gadgets. Is it my impression or shops are selling bigger and bigger stockings? Some of the ideas I found around are:

Make your own bookmarks. Use beautiful photos from magazines, or use computer and graphic software to design a special one with a personalised message. Make a batch and laminate them all in one go. A bookmark can look like a train, a flower, a doll, a ruler or anything you wish to. You could even write a story or message that continues on the back and then again on the front to amuse the recipient of the gift.

Make handkerchiefs. You can use old bed sheets or fabric leftovers in flannel or muslin. If you can embroider them, add a small design or initials.

Make paper dolls. Design your own, or download from the internet, dolls and clothes, colour in and laminate the body and let the children design the clothes for the doll. You can also buy a magazine with the dolls' patterns and then copy, arrange and adjust/clone what you need for perpetual use.

Prepare a colouring book. Look for printable pictures on the net, printing them on good quality paper, and then binding them together with a ribbon.

Bake some special cookies or muffins. They will be much healthier than shop-bought Mars Bars and cookies. Decorate them at home.

Prepare some small bags of goodies: nuts, sultanas, dates, figs, apricots or sesame sticks. Pack them beautifully and add a cinnamon stick for a gorgeous scent!

A way for kids to earn money

Most duties today we pay others to take care of in our homes, during the Great Depression and up to the Sixties were actually performed by children. Those children have now grown up to be responsible, self reliant and hard working people. That's what we would like to raise; a generation that is independent and loves work.

There are plenty of chores that a child can tackle to earn money without getting hurt or being over-tired. A seven year old can probably wash a car or bicycle using a sponge and a bucket, standing on a stool. You save the money you would spend by washing the car at a garage. Next time he will think twice before making doodles on the windows as he remembers how long it took to wash them away.

A child might also be good at vacuuming the car and clearing the seats from any leftover food wrappers, crumbs etc. Again, once he sees how long it takes to catch each crumb, he might think twice before he starts chewing away in your car. So, you will also be teaching good behaviour and responsibility. Once your child has learned to clean the car well and quickly inside and out he has also learned a job; he can use his skills to invite the neighbours for a cheap car wash so he can earn money towards his camping trip with the Scouts or whatever he wants.

There are plenty of other jobs that you can suggest to earn some cash, from cutting the grass, to weeding, tidying up the shed shelf by shelf, washing the windows on the ground floor, wash the entire bathroom from tiles to ceiling, paint the shed, and so on.

Once your children get acquainted with work and save towards something, they learn an important principle which will help them avoid debt in their life - a really good achievement! Then Christmas, birthdays and parties can become something a bit more productive than just spending silly money for a grumpy fellow. The spoiled cousin of Harry Potter does not need a replica in any household.

The principle is, of course, the opposite of what we are told by media and stores every day: *save now, buy later!*

9

CREATING BEAUTIFUL GIFTS OUT OF ORDINARY ITEMS

"You give but little when you give of your possessions. It is when you give of yourself that you truly give." *(Kahlil Gibran, "The Prophet")*

If you are determined not to spend a fortune for birthdays, Christmas etc. you might stretch your mind to find creative solutions to your lack of funds by making good use of two things: some cheap items and your skills. You might be good at carpentry jobs for example. With sand paper and elbow grease, restore the surface of a sturdy old chair or bedroom cabinet. Make it look nice and smooth and then paint it in light washes of pastel colours.

If you are good with stencils you can even use a sponge and dab some colourful decorations onto the back of the chair. You can end up with a beautiful, tasteful product that you can give to a loved one. Or you can check out a book on stained glass from the local library. Learn the techniques, invest in 4 or 5 enamel paints, and then decorate transparent or ceramic items. A cheap way to learn is to make experiments on any transparent plastic container from a shop. You can buy some old drinking glasses or a glass jar from a charity for a few pence. Draw and paint using the stained glass technique, create a unique object, then, when you are happy with the result, donate it to a friend and enjoy their delighted expression.

Any boring container can be decorated using several techniques, from decoupage to papier-mâché, to painting, and then it can be filled with home made truffles or other treats and donated. Use scraps of fabric and lace to make dresses for dolls, covers for prams, and so on. A good Christmas hamper can be prepared by painting an old basket in gold or white, placing some crunched shredded paper (saved from your last purchase of breakable items) and then adding traditional treats such as local honey, fruit conserve, home made Christmas cake, dried flowers, ribbon, dates and nuts. Wrap with cling film, secure with ribbon tape, attach a decoration rescued from your craft box, and you have spent only a minimal amount of money for a warm and inviting gift.

To keep the kids occupied during the festive holidays, you don't need to buy them the themed colouring books with attached felt pens; the books are usually made with low quality paper and the felt pens will also be "cheap and cheerful" and not last at all. Instead, during the year collect decorative items, old cards, seashells, dry flowers etc. in a craft box, which you will present to the kids as a present - not an entitlement.

One time I cut off lots of photos of toys from an old toy catalogue and I gave them to my two year old with a bit of blu-tac. I was amazed at how much time he spent arranging and rearranging them on a chair. You can cut off cartoon characters from cereal boxes or most containers, and then let your children do what they like with them. Or you can get a craft book or website full of ideas and let them follow the instructions.

Another craft that most kids will like is playing with play-dough. Again, it is not necessary to purchase it from a shop - you can find instructions on the internet. You can mix some white flour with water and salt and add some food colourant if needed. The objects made can be dehydrated in an oven or dehydrator and then painted. You will easily fill up an afternoon in this way and you will only spend 50 pence for the flour and salt.

Trading cards are also quite popular among children but can become an expensive habit. A cheaper way to reproduce trading cards is to cut off from magazines and boxes some characters, animals, plants, famous people and so on. Glue them on strong white paper or place them on a laminate sheet arranging them so they can be cut off in rectangular shapes.

With a bit of practice you can make plenty of cards - but don't allow yours to be given away!

Those who are good with plants can also provide a welcome gift without a large expense. It is not too difficult to raise a plant from seed or from cuttings, and when it's looking just right, prepare a decorative container and a card to give to a loved one. There's quite a difference between a shop-bought plant and a home grown one. In the latter one, you have spent time and energy to make the plant grow healthy and strong, you have loved the plant and when you donate it you can make that plant a gift of love. Children love weird plants, so why not try the Dyonaea (venus fly catcher) or Nepentes? They will be engaged for hours just looking at how small insects disappear into those carnivorous plants. And you will save on insect sprays and traps!

10
SAVING ON HOUSEHOLD BILLS

"The greatest discovery of my generation is that a human being can alter his life by altering his attitudes." (William James)

It doesn't matter if we earn £500 a month or a day - those who really want can, with some effort, save some money, electricity and gas and become more self-reliant. Those who are lucky enough to have no debts, and to have saved some money, may want to invest it instead of leaving it in the bank to earn 0.3% interest.

Gold, silver and stock shares are good, if you can forecast market fluctuations; however, solar panels, compost bins, heat pumps and other energy saving devices remain stable in giving you substantial savings over the years while food and energy bills increase at the current rate. For hundreds of tips, look on the internet specific topics such as "how to save on electricity bills" etc. There are UK comparison websites such as USwitch and Moneysupermarket.com (and many others), but be aware that some of these sites get commission for selling a particular brand or offer, so search around carefully.

I just wish to get you started by thinking of where we may save or lose money. Let's review the main points.

Electricity

When replacing kitchen white goods, choose A-rated appliances, which are designed to use less energy and hopefully to last longer. Purchase a washing machine that allows a daily wash at 30°C (85°F). If you have invested in hot water solar panels, connect the washing machine so that it uses the hot water only and 10 minutes after the start, turn down the thermostat so that to do the final rinse the machine will only use cold water. This trick will give you many cheap washes during sunny days in any season.

Solar panels

Twelve years ago my monthly electricity bill was £9 and now is over £30. This is a good time to start saving in any way we can! You may consider installing photovoltaic panels (PV) to produce electricity or hot water solar panels (evacuated tube type), to help with heating the water. PV costs from £5,000 to £12,000 but they will save you a lot in the long run. You might know that electricity generated by your panels can be sent to the grid and sold back to the electricity company, generating some income too.

Solar panels for water production are less expensive, probably costing around £4,000 for a 4-bed house. We have had ours for almost 6 years and we are very satisfied with them. Although we are not in a sunny country or at a beach, in summer we don't need to heat the water unless we want to exceed 50°C (122°F) in a really dark, cloudy day.

On sunny days, the temperature of the panel elements easily reaches over 80°C (175°F) and sometimes goes past 100°C (212°F) - steaming hot stuff! You might think that solar panels are a waste during winter in the UK; however, if the outdoor temperature is for example 10°C (50°F), we can reasonably expect the water to be heated to at least 20-25°C (68-77°F) if the day isn't too dark and gloomy. So, talk to those who already use solar panels of both kinds and gather information on deals, government grants, "feed in tariffs" etc. They might be just what you need to protect yourself from ever raising energy bills, even with the feed in tariff cleverly being reduced by our shortsighted UK Government in 2011.

Heat pumps

Another good idea to consider, in order to lower heating and cooling bills, is heat pumps. They work on the principle of extracting heat and cold from the air or the ground and they may require a large hole to be dug in your garden and lots of changes inside the home, so it's best to do your research well in advance and perhaps as soon as you move house but before you establish a beautiful garden. There are several types of heat pumps and professional advice is recommended before embarking on such an expense.

General savings

Meanwhile, do get used to turning off lights and appliances when not in use - everything adds up. Don't use a tumble dryer to dry your clothes, unless you are desperate. That machine eats electricity like a hungry monster. Instead, put the clothes on a drying rack in the hottest room of the house, or on your radiators, and in 12 hours they should be ready for the heating cupboard. Bed sheets are quite big but you can put them on top of the backs of two chairs - put the chairs six feet apart and hang the bed sheets in between.

A sunny conservatory is also a good place where to dry clothes. To avoid long hours of ironing to smooth out the wrinkles, hang them up neatly, and then maybe encourage some young helpers to earn a star, by folding each item nicely. In Italy, most people can find in local shops a particular type of drying rack, which is fixed to the ceiling of their bathroom. It is approximately 6 or 7 feet long, and with an ingenious device it allows you to load all the clothes and bed sheets; when finished, simply rotate the handle to lift them to the ceiling, and out of your way.

Several years ago we bought one in Italy for less than £15, and brought it back via airplane. Our long and thin box had no problems at the check-in point, and was loaded together with skis, bikes and other odd shaped belongings from other customers. Oddly, over here in the UK you can only buy some smaller types. Even Ikea doesn't provide a decent one which is the same.

Another way of saving is to avoid buying certain types of "economy" items, as they are useless or break right away. Just as an example, when you try out Tesco Economy range for washing up gloves, you will be wasting your money. The fingers immediately curl up and get stuck to themselves in folds, resulting in a treacherous experience when trying to put them on. When you try to extend the stuck plastic, you simply can't do it and end up throwing away such gloves in frustration.

The same is true for Tesco Value Glue Sticks. They feature a super-wobbly stick that simply doesn't glue anything, and as you *have to* buy a set of them you are throwing away your money, and become frustrated. Sorry for picking on Tesco all the time, but I live near a Tesco store and not other supermarkets or I would give you a wider range of rip-off examples!

In conclusion, always test products before assuming that they will save you money; sometimes spending more means saving, too.

Gas heating

It seems obvious to some, but the first thing to remember in winter is that we need to dress for the season, not for the beach. It's not very good to wear a t-shirt in an over heated house in January, when the outside temperature is between 2° and 10°C (35-50°F). Moreover, contrary to what people believe, you don't need to reach 20°C (68°F) with your heating system - don't we cope with summer clothes during our British summers with an average temperature of 17°C (63°F)? So, let's lower the thermostat, and wear cord or velvet trousers, thicker shirts, long sleeves, double layers, and wool jumpers and we certainly won't be freezing at 18°C (65°F). The second, obvious thing is to keep moving to keep warm or to have a hot water bottle and a blanket if we are planning to sit. Washing windows, vacuuming, ironing, cooking and mopping floors are excellent ways to kick-start your circulation and feel warm inside out. So, next time somebody complains about the dreadfully cold temperature of 18°C (65°F) while going around wearing a skimpy t-shirt, torn jeans and bare feet, you may wish to hand him or her the mop and thank him for volunteering to mop the floors. Chances are that the complainer might grab his jumper really fast, and stop hassling you!

If your funds are sufficient, replace single glazed windows with double glazed ones as they save a lot of heat. There are government grants for loft insulation and cavity wall insulation and insulating the hot water tank is also quite cheap and easy. Eating warm food, a hearty soup, or a warm herbal tea, also helps to feel more comfortable without setting the heating at a really high temperature.

Hard Water

In some areas in the UK the water is really "hard"; you might have noticed that your skin is itchy after washing, or that there is a limescale deposit on all your appliances. That deposit also slows down the water flow in the pipes and makes the heating system less efficient. Even your kettle will not perform well and your washing machine will suffer. Glasses and containers always look dirty when limescale dries up on them. Taps will eventually start dripping, you will tighten them up more and more, and eventually the continuous "drip-drip" will require a new valve and a hefty bill from the plumber and the water company. Hard water also requires more soap and shampoo for lathering, more detergent, and more washing up liquid. And none of these products are cheap!

There are lots of products on sale that are supposed to deal with this problem and I am personally considering at least two solutions. One is to replace all the taps with lever operated mixer taps (and ceramic valves) so that I will never have to tighten them again. This will also give me the chance to use warm water instead of freezing or burning, and save some money.

The other solution is to purchase and install a salt-based water softening system. A good plumber can install such a system from about £500 and although this is quite an expense, it will save my money in the future so I consider it an investment worth saving for. I must say that after washing my hair in hard water for years, when I go abroad I really enjoy the silky feel of my hair thanks to softer water.

You might also wish to install a filtering system under your kitchen sink for your tap water so you can drink safe, purified and tasty water. This tastes as good as shop-bought water and will be much cheaper than buying bottles all the time. It also gives you some independence as at times we saw certain items disappearing from supermarkets shelves within hours and water is something you want to have all the time.

Saving water without compromising hygiene

It is wise to consider if a saving we are making is actually causing a problem in a different area of our life. Water consumption is always much higher than we think but it can be reduced to save money every day, while keeping good hygiene standards. One easy way to save water is to swap baths for quick showers. You only need about 3 minutes to wash and rinse your body. All the rest is luxury. Step out, get dry, put some clothes on and only then wash your hair, if you can cope with bending down. You will save another 8-10 minutes of running water and while you are lathering your hair you can turn off the tap without feeling cold.

When using water in the kitchen or bathroom, teach your loved ones to avoid leaving the tap open unless they are actually using it. It's amazing how much clean water goes down the drain while we brush our teeth or pick up the next plate to rinse.

Water your plants using a water-butt instead of tap water which is chlorinated and therefore quite harsh on them.

Another way of saving water is to change the way we wash our car. Instead of spending half an hour with a hosepipe, we could try the old method of a bowl of water and a sponge, followed by a rinse in the end with a clean bowl. Children love washing cars! Teach them how to do it properly and save more money by giving them a tip instead of the local garage.

Washing our hands often should not be regarded as wasting water, as it is a good precaution against the spread of disease (which is costly and difficult to cope with). Cross contamination is a guaranteed way of spreading germs all over the house, and there is nothing less safe than a dirty fridge, as we become contaminated by touching it and then transfer the germs onto the food we pick up. Cross contamination is also a major problem when doing the washing up and putting washed items away.

Rinsed dishes are safer and cheaper than soapy ones

I hope you will allow me to be quite frank and not be offended by the quotes and statistics below. I have researched this topic as well as I could. Washing dishes (meaning dishes, cutlery, chopping boards, glasses, mugs, pots, pans etc.) requires very little hot water if one scrubs the food out of the dishes well before washing them and doesn't delay washing up for hours. Some people cover the dishes with soap and then put them to dry on the rack, or wipe them with a tea towel. They might think that their effort is enough, and that they are saving water by not rinsing. Bless you for your efforts to save the Planet. However, I hope that you will re-direct your efforts to safer enterprises. Would you wash your hair with shampoo and then dry it with a towel, without rinsing first? No? There is no difference with dishes. Unless they are rinsed with water, they are *not* clean, nor safe to use. It should be quite obvious: we rinse after washing our face, hands and clothes, so we should rinse dishes, cutlery etc.

You will find that when you get in contact with foreigners, they will be shocked to learn that many people in the UK, Australia and Holland don't rinse their dishes and cutlery. Actually, the topic is a very hot one among many forums in the UK. If you don't rinse the dishes, you are not actually saving much water. All you are achieving is to spread all the dirt, germs and toxic chemicals onto the drying rack, only to pick them up later with a tea towel, which will transfer more germs from each utensil to the other, ready to grow. Gross!

Washing up liquids are supposed to remove the bacteria from the oily part of an item, then a water rinse should remove cleaning agent, germs and any residual dirt. One single bacteria, left on any wet surface, multiplies at a steady rate, and in 6 hours will have created enough offspring to make you ill: 16,777,216 of them to be precise.

Anything not properly rinsed will look, smell and feel slimy and greasy. It helps to keep in mind that bacteria such as Salmonella and Escherichia coli, survive towel or air-drying on dishes and *after towel-drying the cloth becomes contaminated*. They thrive and grow on these surfaces. Salmonella can survive in washed and rinsed dishes, if they are not immersed in bleach for disinfection afterwards. Be careful if you feed raw meat to your pets! For some individuals even contact with just ten organisms are enough to develop severe disease. Rinsing dishes will allow you to eat tastier foods, too - no soapy taste! Your kitchen towels won't need changing every day and food poisoning events will mostly be restricted to when you are watching gross kitchens in "How clean is your house?"

We don't skimp on health and safety just to save a few pennies. An estimated 2 million people in the UK develop food-borne illnesses every year. And not all of them have eaten in a dirty restaurant (as most restaurants use dish washers and sanitize dishes with bleach). Recent studies suggest, in fact, that you are much more likely to get food poisoning from eating at home.

Sometimes people suffer from regular mild food poisoning and don't realise it, thinking that their illness, or continuous trips to the toilet, are caused by a cold or something similar. Such sicknesses cost money for all the days that we lose at work and school, for childcare etc. Most can easily be avoided by keeping hands, bathrooms, kitchens and utensils clean and rinsed. So, rinse, rinse, rinse. Save the water in areas where your guests' health and yours are not put at risk.

In a BBC article linked below, the topic is washing up; in the article there is an interesting statement we ought to consider. Washing up liquids contain chemicals that mimic the female hormone, oestrogen. Try to wear rubber gloves, or these hormone replicas will penetrate your skin, with obvious consequences. (Maybe a really high-pitched voice?) Rinsing is important, says the article. Washing-up liquids are also harsh and poisonous. If you drink them in relatively small quantities, they will make you ill; but in large quantities they will actually kill you. How many people swallow minute quantities of dishwashing liquid with their food and drink, because traces are left on their dishes and cutlery, after they've been washed - but not rinsed with water?

Maybe somebody should start a nation-wide campaign to re-educate the public regarding the need of having clean and rinsed dishes, starting from primary schools onward. This should reduce hospital admissions, food poisoning deaths, doctors visits and sickness at work: another way of saving money, having a sparkly kitchen and being healthier! The topic is closed! Phew!

Sources:

http://www.ncbi.nlm.nih.gov/pmc/articles/PMC1555674
http://answers.google.com/answers/threadview/id/248104.html
http://www.nursinginpractice.com/article/295/Washing_those_dirty_di
shes_in_public_and_in_private
http://www.wikihow.com/Wash-Dishes
http://www.bbc.co.uk/dna/h2g2/A337006

Alternative ways of heating the house

Many years ago, every house had a fireplace in most rooms including bedrooms; people would cook on the fire and hot coals or ashes were kept near the beds in metallic containers to warm up the room. Nowadays, many people are re-discovering Aga cookers, wood burners and open fireplaces. While an open fireplace has an aesthetic value, a wood burner is more efficient in distributing the heat in the right direction, and in comparison burns less wood or coal to produce more heat.

Some wood burners have a dedicated area on top, where it is possible to put a pot and cook a meal, too. If you have enough funds, you can invest in a wood/coal burner, and warm up your room when you wish to; wood costs less than gas and prices don't increase by 20% a year. A trained installer will help you to choose the correct size of wood burner, depending on the size of the room you want to heat. There will be expenses for a lined flue pipe and some brickwork, and chimney sweeping costs, if there is an old chimney there. I would expect the cost of building fireplace and chimney from scratch to be quite high so this option is not open for everybody. However, it would be good to save towards installing a wood burner. This device also creates a cosy, welcoming atmosphere, ideal for those who love to curl up with a good book, during a winter evening.

Another interesting piece of equipment to consider is an Aga cooker (and its competitors). The AGA cooker is a stored-heat stove and cooker invented in 1929 by the Nobel Prize-winning Swedish physicist Gustaf Dalén. It is quite expensive and not as energy efficient as some other cookers/heaters, so I recommend you do your own research before you make any decision.

Cleaning the home with home-made products

There is no need to purchase a different cleaner for each surface of the house. You can make your own cleaners with baking soda, lemon and white vinegar. They are cheaper than branded products and not toxic. A cleaner suitable for any surface is simply made by mixing ½ cup (120ml) vinegar and ¼ cup (60ml) baking soda into 4 pints (2 litres) of water. This product removes water stains in bathrooms really well. To clean stainless steel use a cloth dampened with undiluted white vinegar, or olive oil. Wipe dry using a clean cloth. Scouring powder: for top of stove or refrigerator use baking soda directly applied with a damp sponge. To remove stickers, sponge vinegar over them several times, and wait 15 minutes, then rub off the stickers.

For more tips, look on the internet using keywords such as "home made cleaning products". You will be pleased to find out how many uses there are, for the three ingredients mentioned in the mixes. You can purchase vinegar, baking soda and salt in large containers and save even more money. Salt is more scarce and expensive during times of ice and snow, when reserves are low and imports from abroad cause its price to rise substantially.

11
HOME MADE MEALS VERSUS CONVENIENCE FOOD

"The most remarkable thing about my mother is that for thirty years she served the family nothing but leftovers. The original meal has never been found." (Calvin Trillin)

What happened to the mother of Mr. Trillin could hardly happen today as we consume so many ready meals that one couldn't possibly find any leftovers. OK, I admit it; I think that to fight our way out of recession we can learn how to cook from scratch and do it as much as possible. A good search for inspiring recipes or saving tips on the internet will definitely get you millions of ideas - but how many of those suggestions will you remember when the computer is off? So, let's get started with some basic principles. All we need is to focus on real nutrition (the base for optimal health) while keeping an eye on hidden costs. The easiest way to save money in the kitchen is to cook from scratch as often as possible! But firstly, let's talk about the "other" food.

Convenience food

"How can a society that exists on instant mashed potatoes, packaged cake mixes, frozen dinners, and instant cameras teach patience to its young?" (Paul Sweeney)

In our supermarkets, there is an endless choice of ready meals for every taste - Busy parents buy them during the day, and younger people in the evening. When I go there at around 7pm. I usually meet lots of young people. They are all looking for ready meals for the night. Surely they have some staples in their homes? Some fruit and vegetables in their fridge? Apparently, this is not the case.

All I see at the tills is food ready for the oven or microwave. I imagine these customers have a low paid job or a student loan and big dreams for their future. Has any of them sat down and calculated how long they will take to repay their debt or a future mortgage at this rate of spending?

Because I tell you - convenience food is not *that* convenient, financially speaking. That's right - you read well. Oh, I agree it is very convenient for somebody else. Food companies want to make money but as raw products (fruit, vegetables, milk, meat) are too cheap, they process them as much as possible to "add value"- and raise the price. Then they add some clever packaging, with various health or taste claims, and through some smart marketing campaigns, reach the appropriate public to let them know how they can be healthy and happy with such time savers.

Viewers get used to see brand images and when they go to our local stores, many of them recognise the brand as familiar and therefore trust worthy and purchase it like pre-programmed machines. Marketing people are indeed experts in psychology and in manipulating our mind, easing it to the concept that we "need" a product. However, when we do our maths, convenience food is everything but convenient. You don't believe me? Pick up your calculator then. I will show you what I mean.

- ✓ Bag of Tesco frozen mashed potatoes: £2.00/kg.
- ✓ Weight: 650 grams
- ✓ Price: £1.30

- ✓ Bag of raw potatoes: 0.54/kg
- ✓ Weight 2.5 kg
- ✓ Price: £1.35

So, by adding 5p you can buy almost *four times more* product. You are spending £1.46 more for the ready product. When you buy processed food, you pay for time, packaging, advertising and overhead costs and you have a limited amount of food. This is very expensive, especially if you are feeding three or four people in this way. We often save ourselves the hassle of 10-20 minutes of work, by paying four times more for the product. This explains why some people's grocery bills are a bit too high.

Ready pasta dishes are very popular but overly priced, if you are hoping to make savings. Consider the following: if you buy a pack of pasta, some canned tomatoes, one clove of garlic and one onion you can prepare and serve a delicious meal for five people in 25 minutes, spending £1, equivalent to 20 pence per person. In comparison, one Tesco Goodness Tomato Pasta Twists Snack Pot (200g) costs 50 pence/100 grams, (£5/kg.) Now let's do the super-maths.

✓ Home made pasta dish: 20 pence per serving.

✓ Ready made pasta dish: £1.00 per serving.

That's five times more expensive than making it yourself. Do you call this *convenience* food? Perhaps it is very convenient indeed - for the supermarkets that cash in our negative attitude about cooking from scratch. This reasoning applies to most processed foods including pizza, bread, biscuits, cakes, sandwiches and baby foods. For the price of the average sandwich (£1.80-2.20) I can easily buy a whole loaf of bread and a filler. If one is serious about getting out of debt, and perhaps eating higher quality food, the very first thing that needs to go is processed food. It really makes a difference for your pocket in the long run.

✓ Buy ready pasta for 21 days a month: £21

✓ Make your pasta for 21 days a month: £4.20

✓ Savings: £16.80

This is well over £200 a year. If you start adding drinks, crisps and a dessert you will see how you can save a large amount of money by preparing your own meals at home and taking them wherever you go. Of course - you are a very busy person and don't have any time to cook. Surely, if you start work at 8am, and return home at 9pm., it is difficult to do much work. But most people return home much earlier. And sometimes, it's our attitude that makes a difference.

Most inexperienced cooks believe that cooking from scratch takes several hours. They would rather spend their free time doing something else. But if you actually learn 2 or 3 basic recipes - say one based on rice, one on pasta and one on veggies - then cooking from scratch takes about half an hour or less for most meals and perhaps two hours for very elaborate preparations and 3 courses meals for 5 guests. It's all about attitude, priorities, practice, and a touch of organisation and good planning.

This means that if you enter the kitchen at 6:30pm with a clear idea of what your meal will be, within half an hour you can be sitting and enjoying a home made plate of delicious food, which will not cost you the earth. There are plenty of useful semi-processed foods such as frozen peas, frozen corn, dehydrated fruit and veggies etc., which may be used successfully to prepare some good meals. However, there are entire meals prepared by the industry, which simply don't help nutritionally or financially so we can choose in which proportion we want them to be part of our diet and accept the consequences. So, if you find yourself eating ready meals at every mealtime, now you know where your money is going. Try to reduce ready meals to once or twice a week and taste the difference!

The silver lining of cooking from scratch is that you will eat a tastier, cheaper, nutritious meal and you won't have to throw in the bin a large quantity of plastic containers, wrappers and carton packaging. Until about forty years ago, there was no need for rubbish collection as nobody would have been so mad to throw food or anything in the bin, and anything else would have been burnt, reused or recycled until it was literally consumed.

How did our grandparents make it through the war and the Great Depression? They were thrifty, they worked hard, and they cooked from scratch. People have cooked from scratch for thousands of years - why are we suddenly avoiding the wonderful art of cooking? Let's bring back the pleasure of a good, hearty meal to our tables: it might help the purse and the waist line and bring enjoyment to every meal.

Planning meals ahead

Some people like the idea of planning ahead what they will cook. They choose what they fancy eating, prepare the shopping list and buy exactly what's needed. They don't have to throw away any food; they save money and often maintain a healthier diet as it is not based on costly last minute processed foods.

If you would like the idea, you can involve your family in planning and preparing the meals. Try Tesco's online meal planner, at www.tescorealfood.com. Simply select the number of days, type of meal, favourite ingredients, number of people, budget and time allocated for cooking. You can print and share online your recipes and even have the needed ingredients delivered to your door if convenient.

You might think that spending £3 or £4 for delivery is not saving you money, however, if you are an impulsive buyer who simply can't stick to a shopping list, a delivery could actually be a money saver! Be warned, this is a very addictive meal planner as it can produce a stunning-looking meal plan with photos within 20 seconds so you might end up playing with it for longer than needed!

Preparing things in advance.

To save time and money we can prepare some foods in advance for later use. For example, we can prepare a dish based on pasta, rice or couscous, and put it in a sealed container to take to work. That will save us quite a lot of money in the long run. We can make our own lasagne or bread, and freeze them for another day. If you use lots of tomato sauce, make a batch of it to use for a few days instead of buying expensive ready-made sauces. You can also freeze it in cubes so you can use it in small quantity to add a tomato taste to a particular dish. Soups can be frozen in cubes, too. The possibilities are endless.

A homemade fruit salad is always cheaper than a shop bought one. One can prepare his own sandwiches in the night for the following day and be creative with leftovers. Peanuts, cashew nuts, dates and sultanas are a great snack, of much greater nutritional value than a bag of crisps or a milk chocolate bar loaded with sugar. Buy them in bulk from internet health stores to save money, and avoid the salt laden varieties.

Another way to save time and money is to slice a generous amount of vegetables (onions, mushrooms, garlic) and freeze them in small packages so when a stir-fry or casserole is needed we have much of our vegetables ready.

If you have prepared too much food one day, freeze the leftovers and one day you will be glad they are available if you are too tired to cook. If you are fortunate enough to have a dehydrator, did you know that you can dehydrate most meals and keep them in perfect condition for a long time? There is a whole area dedicated to dehydration in this book so you can consider this appliance as a possible investment.

More ways of saving money in the kitchen

✓ There are hundreds of tips that you can find easily on the internet on how to save. Replace meat dishes with pulses such as beans, peas and lentils.

✓ Make your own ice-lollies by freezing your 100% fruit smoothies in dedicated moulds.

✓ Put less prawns and seafood in a stir-fry for pasta, and add instead a teaspoon of fish sauce to give a "sea" flavour to the dish.

✓ Use half meat, half wheat/barley/oats or veggies in meatballs to have a cheaper, filling dish.

✓ Use grape juice instead of wine for drinks: it is much cheaper, you don't need to be 18 to buy it, it contains all the goodness of vitamins, antioxidants etc. and not the alcohol which will slowly destroy your liver and force you to have unpaid days off work with a hangover!

✓ Grow your food (see gardening section) and meet fellow gardeners for swaps of any excess produce.

✓ Save some food in your pantry for rainy days: buy when on offer and store away. (See food storage section in this book)

✓ Make your own cakes and biscuits if you really have to eat them!

✓ Make your own pizza and add your favourite toppings choosing among your homegrown vegetables. It takes only 10 minutes to prepare the dough!

Learn tons of skills from www.makeitandmendit.com (home, food, garden, interiors, DIY, fashion). Learn how to preserve fruit and vegetables in jars (canning). It all boils down to cleaning, cutting, cooking and sterilising and once you have learned the principles, the possibilities are endless and the savings substantial. John Seymour, the father of self-sufficiency, said, "Nothing should be wasted on the self-sufficient holding. The dustman should never have to call." If you want to learn skills ranging from gardening to spinning, curing, preserving, raising animals, pressing oil, preparing apple cider vinegar and much more, look in my links and book list for John Seymour's book details. It is well worth reading everything he wrote.

12
WHOLE GRAINS AND SPROUTS AS HEALTHY MONEY SAVERS

"The discovery of a new dish does more for the happiness of mankind than the discovery of a star." (Anthelme Brillat-Savarin)

Let's talk about how whole grains may help us to save money and be healthier, how to cook with very little gas or electricity, and how our body deals with nutrients or lack of them. There are two main types of grains: whole grains (meaning, whole, intact, natural, unprocessed) and refined grains (which means that they have been processed and one of their layers or parts has been removed). Refined wheat for example is used to make refined flour, (known as white or all-purpose flour) which is then used to bake most cakes, biscuits and breads.

It is useful to know that once we eliminate the outer layer of the wheat kernel, (bran), and the inner part (germ), most of the nutrition of a kernel of wheat is gone for good. In fact we lose precious fibre by eliminating the bran and a host of vitamins and minerals by eliminating the germ. I am simplifying things a lot here, but there are thousands of websites that can explain the concept in detail if you are interested.

Once a kernel of grain has been refined and used to create processed food in the form of white flour, it needs preservatives to survive on shop shelves for a long time, and vitamins added to compensate for the ones lost during the milling process. However, while the vitamins that were originally contained in this little grain were organic, whole, and live, and came in their original "nature package" with useful fibre, it is not so for added vitamins.

Those are instead chemical substances replicated from the natural ones, or extracted and isolated from natural sources, they are inorganic and they are not complete. For example, vitamin C as found in nature has a long list of "ingredients" while synthetic vitamin C (ascorbic acid) contains only 4 or 5 of the original components. So, eating whole grains as opposed to refined grains is much healthier in the long run. Next time you pick up a box of cereals which reads "Fortified grains", read instead "stripped of organic vitamins, and then chemically injected with inorganic stuff" or quite simply, read "not so healthy".

Now let's talk about whole grains, such as wheat, barley, buckwheat (which is actually a grass) spelt, amaranth and quinoa. These are just some of the whole grains that we can add to our daily meals to enrich them. Because they are whole they can fill you up nicely for hours, they give you slow-release energy and their fibre is welcomed by our digestive system, usually overworked by dense and heavy foods.

Eating wholemeal bread instead of white bread makes a world of difference for our taste buds, our health and for prevention of diseases. As wholemeal bread is more filling, you will need to eat less wholemeal than white bread to feel satisfied, so in the long term you are saving money on many levels.

Many commercial "wholemeal" breads contain a maximum 17% wholemeal flour and the rest is white flour. To work out what's the difference, ask your local baker if he has any 100% wholemeal bread and you will see a much denser, heavier product than the one you are used to. In most supermarkets the bakers can show you a full list of ingredients for all their normal and specialty breads. If the bread you buy is quite sweet it may contain fructose, which, according to Robert H. Lustig, MD, "has increased coincidentally with the worldwide epidemics of obesity and metabolic syndrome." (See link at the end of this section)

Make your own wholemeal bread and see how different it is from the white baguette you buy at the store. A basic healthy bread mix contains flour, water, salt, a sprinkle of honey, oil and yeast, and is put in the heated oven - making bread is an art but it is very simple to learn. A six year old can easily master making a basic bread loaf in one lesson, so can you.

Eating cakes made with refined flour (99% are not whole meal) is a double suicide for your immune system. By consuming refined flour mixed with refined sugar, you are sending to your pancreas a high level of sugars and the poor organ suddenly needs to pump a lot of insulin in the blood to compensate for the sugar peak. When the sugar level goes down again, you will feel headache, tiredness and cravings for sweets and you might eat more refined flour/sugar and create the vicious circle again.

But the body is still looking for its building blocks (natural, organic vitamins, proteins, minerals etc.) and it can't find them in refined, processed food. So you eat and eat but you are constantly hungry. This might create several problems in the long run, starting at diabetes, weight issues and depression, then joint pains. Health issues can be very expensive to deal with. You might eat a whole package of biscuits full of refined sugar and flour, preservatives and colourants, but I bet you won't feel energetic and bouncy at all. In fact, you might even feel depressed and automatically reach for more! Try instead slow energy-releasing carbohydrates such as whole grains and wholemeal flours, when choosing breads and the occasional cake. Choose molasses instead of refined sugar: it contains easily absorbed iron and lots of useful minerals because molasses is unrefined sugar in its primitive stage.

Refined sugar only gives you empty calories and no nutrients: that's why it makes you always feel hungry and your mood can swing up and down until the next "fix". Aspartame achieves the same effect and it's a poison to your body, too. Sugar lowers your immune system defences and is a major factor behind the obesity and cancer epidemic that is currently thriving in industrialised countries where consumption of processed and sugary foods is high.

A bit of experimenting can help with changing a sweet tooth craving by introducing natural foods in every day meals. Any soup will have a heartier taste and consistency if you add some whole grains to it, from oats to wheat, barley or couscous, the choice is great. The nutrients will be absorbed by your digestive system and gratefully sent around to nourish each cell of your body. The bran will go to your stomach and intestine to create a soft mixture that will not remain stuck in your digestive system releasing toxins; those toxins need to find a way out or they will make you feel tired and ill all the time.

Overall, choosing whole foods will always be a positive step in any diet and help you to live within your means. Not only, but eating whole grains (along with fresh fruits and vegetables) can greatly help in avoiding constipation, a problem that challenges the majority of people in modern society and according to many experts is the cause of a host of health problems.

Doctor Lustig is a great speaker, with a clear and charming presentation style that you will love. For an in-depth explanation of the causes of metabolic disease go here: www.youtube.com/watch?v=dBnniua6-oM or search for UCtelevision channel on YouTube

The Wonder Box

Of course, we'd love to cook whole grains with the lowest possible use of energy; either we can use a pressure cooker or a slow cooker. But to use very little energy, we need a Wonder Box (or hay box). You will find thousands of instructions and photos on the internet if you enter into your search engine the words "wonder box recipes". Wonder box cooking is not restricted only to Boy Scouts or Victorian times. It's a very clever way of cooking something in a super insulated container from which the heat simply cannot escape. You can cook bread and casseroles, and of course all your soups with a wonder box. And when you have finished, you have a lovely warm blanket to wrap yourself with!

You don't need any special equipment to make a Wonder Box yourself. If you have a carton box, a normal cooking pot with a tight fitting lid and a few blankets or even some old coats you will be just fine. Let's see how you can cook things this way.

If we pick up a bag of barley, the instructions on the bag will call for 60 to 90 minute on the hob. No way! Ten minutes are enough with a wonder box. Simply put 100 grams of barley in a pot filled with boiling water and cook for 10 minutes in the evening. Then turn off the gas, but keep the lid on. Put the hot pot in the carton box and wrap it really carefully with your blankets, so that the heat cannot escape. Close the box and put something on it to keep it firmly closed.

In the morning, open the box, then the pot, and check if the grains are ready. As long as barley has been in warm water for 8 hours, it will be well cooked. Cooking time varies depending on temperature, insulation, quantity of liquid etc. so it's worth doing your own experiments and taking some notes.

Once you have perfected your timing and temperatures, you can use grains cooked overnight for a cheap and filling breakfast. Once drained, they can be reheated and mixed with any of the following: a bit of honey, cinnamon, cocoa powder, sultanas, dried fruit and nuts for a delicious breakfast. You don't have to add dairy milk to them; other options are soy/rice/coconut milk, herbal tea or fruit juice.

Try to have some cooked grains for breakfast instead of your usual sugary cereals. Or maybe add some veggies. You will notice the difference soon. Your ups and downs in energy levels and mood swings will soon ease. You won't be starving by 9:30am. and you won't crave much sugar - all good stuff there. Oh, and by the way, whole grains are much cheaper than processed breakfast cereals! A 15 kg (33lbs) bag of wheat costs £8 at my local farmer - while 1 kg (2.2lbs) of bulgur wheat in any supermarket will be £1-1.50. Maths matters!

What if I am allergic to wheat or gluten?

If you are allergic to wheat, don't cook it. Just sprout it for 2-3 days and it will become a grass with no gluten and no allergens. It will be perfectly chewable and taste like grass. (But not gross!) Did you know that wheatgrass contains a really high level of vitamins? It is an amazing source of health, and much cheaper than vitamin tablets full of chemicals and inorganic substances. This is a vibrant, live food and it will give you lots of energy. Its chemical composition is extremely similar to haemoglobin, the substance that gives the red colour to your red blood cells. But now you will ask me "how do you sprout wheat?" - so let's move to the next part.

How to sprout seeds and grains at home

Many people enjoy a nice Chinese stir-fry once in a while - this tasty dish usually contains long shoots called bean sprouts. You can either buy a small bag of them for about 50 pence, or you can sprout your own and have a fresh supply every day. Not only you will save money, but also you will learn a good skill and have free vitamins - no more need for chemical supplements!

Sprouts can be used in: salads, breads, soups, sandwiches, omelettes, Chinese or Mexican food, casseroles, meatloaf, blended drinks or all by themselves. All you have to do to sprout grains and seeds is to soak them, rinse them, keep them wet and eat them when ready, usually in 3 to 5 days. Most vegetables are safe to be sprouted, however, tomato, pepper or potato seeds are poisonous and fruit sprouts are not supposed to be eaten, either. Sprouting containers need to be hygienically clean and disinfected often, to avoid the risk of Salmonella.

Step one: pick up a handful of seeds and soak them in water for 8-12 hours (overnight is the easiest way) in a small container made of plastic, glass or other material. The seeds are dormant, but when in contact with water they will be revived and start to swell up. Rye, wheat and beans need 12 hours of soaking.

Step two: rinse the seeds with cool water, eliminating any debris or dirt.

Step three: drain the seeds twice a day using a fine wire strainer or a sprouter. You want to keep them moist, not soggy. Keep them in their container and ensure you don't make them soak in water after the first day or they will quickly deteriorate.

Step four: repeat the rinsing and draining for 2-5 days. You will see some tiny little "tails" coming out of your seeds. When the sprouts are as long as the seeds they are ready to eat. If you have far too many sprouts, save them in the refrigerator making sure they stay dry or they will turn brown. A sealed bag will do the trick and will keep them in a good condition for a maximum of five days. You don't need any expensive equipment to sprout seeds and grains. However, if you like doing it often you may want to invest £15 to £20 in a sprouter. This is a circular or rectangular plastic or metallic container with a lid and a colander-type bottom, which makes it easier to do the washing and rinsing. You can buy a sprouter from health food stores and on the internet.

What are the best sprouts for my health?

Alfalfa, broccoli, buckwheat, lentils, mung beans, radish, soybeans, wheat. Avoid gardening seeds as they are treated with chemicals. Again: do not sprout any fruit seeds: they are toxic and some can do serious harm when eaten.

Where do I store my seeds and for how long?

If you store them in a cool, dry and dark place, seeds will last 2-5 years. Humidity should not exceed 60%. Freezing increases their life 4-5 times and refrigerating will double it. However, wheat will easily sprout even after 20 years!

13
DEHYDRATING TO PRESERVE YOUR FOOD

"The preparation of good food is merely another expression of art, one of the joys of civilized living." (Dione Lucas)

A dehydrator is a device that allows you to cook at low temperatures but also to dehydrate food so perfectly that you can store it for a long time. Not only that, but it can be used to create new meals, home made ready meals (soups, cereal bars, snacks, breads) and to prepare raw foods, as it never destroys the enzymes contained in food. Therefore, if you have the desire to try something new and invest a bit of money, you might want to try dehydrating your own foods. We eat dried food often without realising it: dried fruits such as sultanas, dates and bananas have not been cooked but dehydrated industrially. Sage and onion stuffing, culinary herbs, teas, certain types of mushrooms, ready soups, couscous dishes, pasta, lasagne, sauces and cake mixes are also dehydrated. Meat, eggs and milk can also be dehydrated, but as they are animal products they must be handled with care to avoid bacteria growth. Some cereal bars and energy bars are also pressed and dehydrated, not cooked.

While in the U.S.A. most people can find a dehydrator in normal shops and in large supermarkets such as Wal-Mart, over here in the UK only online stores seem to supply them. A dehydrator is not a necessity for a family, so don't worry if you don't have one! However, once you have it, it can become addictive in a positive way. I find it very useful.

How does it work?

It's basically a small, portable "oven" that works by heating air to a constant warm temperature, conveying this air around the food, and making all the water evaporate so you are left with dry food, which can be stored for years in dedicated containers.

There are solar dehydrators (ideal for sunny countries) and electric ones (ideal for the UK!). They weigh around 5-10 kg depending on model and are offered in two designs: either cylindrical (such as Ronco, Ezidri) or Rectangular - similar to a big microwave oven (such as Excalibur, Cabela).

Dehydrators tend to be produced mostly outside of Europe and to be cheaper in the U.S.A., however we have some importers to the UK so there shouldn't be a problem for repairs as dehydrators have very little that can go wrong in them, which is good.

All dehydrators have several stackable, washable trays where the food, which is usually sliced thinly, is placed evenly for a certain amount of hours (usually 8-12) until ready. Some models come with only 5 trays but you can extend to 10 more and just stack them on top of one another.

These machines are quiet to use, apart from the tiny noise of the air coming out, which doesn't really disturb us. A good thing about this warm air is that it becomes useful in winter! And of course the smell that comes out can also be outrageously yummy, especially when drying ripe tomatoes or strawberries.

Prices vary from £99 to more than £180 so it's not a huge expense but they will easily function for 15 to 20 years; if you have cheaper electricity at night they are absolutely a must, although they don't use much electricity any way. An Excalibur with 5 trays uses 400w, so the running cost is approximately 10p for the standard rate for four hours. (Prices change depending on electricity supplier, type of contract and yearly price increases).

How do you use them?

It's quite simple; there are detailed instruction books, but anyway just slice fruit or veggies to achieve slices of 2 mm, spread them evenly on the tray and keep going until all the food is sliced and ready to be dehydrated. Then plug in/turn on and set the temperature to medium (for most foods), low for herbs and high for meat. That's it. It's easier to set the dehydrator before going to bed and when you wake up everything is ready. When the food is dry, it can be eaten right away, or saved in special vacuum bags containing a valve that doesn't let air in, or in airtight jars for the purpose. Or you can invest some £70 in a vacuum-sealing machine and do a really professional job. Sometimes foods are dried for later use but they need to be re-hydrated by adding water (for example pasta dishes, jams etc.)

Useful accessories for the preparation of fruit and vegetable roll-ups

The Excalibur comes with rectangular teflon sheets and the Ezidri with a similar, circular sheet. They can be used for liquid foods, to make fruit leathers. This is a cool way to prepare a super quick, healthy snack based on fruit. It's called "fruit roll up". Simply pour a fruit smoothie on a tray covered with a teflon sheet, and leave to dehydrate for about 8 hours at medium temperature. You are warned: the scent will tempt you all night long. In the morning you will find a soft, pliable disc that you can roll, cut in pieces, shred or use as an omelette. You can wrap it in cling film or oven paper and take it with you. It should last for a long while. However, usually my fruit wraps only last until my kids find out I have prepared them! (An hour on a good day!)

Not only fruit can be used but also savoury "omelette" type wraps can be made using veggies, flax seeds etc. You will be surprised to know that with a dehydrator you can also prepare Ezekiel bread and lots of raw breads and chips, including tortilla chips.

Create your very own "ready meals" cheaply

You can also use these clever machines to save up food when you have made too much and throwing it away doesn't make sense. Simply spread it on the tray and leave it until dry, then pack it and seal it. This works for rice, pasta, couscous, soup, vegetables etc. Instead of buying frozen ready meals you can choose your ingredients and quantities and be creative.

Regarding soups, you can prepare a soup roll up, make it really dry and brittle, then put it in a good blender to powder it and then store it. If you are good at cooking you can create your very own range of foods, pack them, label them and give them as a gift.

Dehydrate your own herbs and spices

If you have a garden or a few pots on the windowsill, and too much parsley or mint etc. you can dehydrate the herbs on a low temperature and save them in dark painted glass containers for later use. Garlic and onions can be dehydrated, ground in the blender and then stored.

Crisp up foods that were becoming a bit soggy or floppy

If you have any cereals, corn tortillas, bread croutons or crisps that were losing their crispiness, you can always pop them on a tray while the dehydrator is going for something else, and they will be nice and crisp again in no time!

Improve the taste of boring fruit, intensify any flavour

If you buy a bag of six apples and quickly realise that they are completely tasteless or even sour, simply slice them, sprinkle them with cinnamon and dehydrate them to eat as a snack. As they have lost their water they will have a more intense and sweeter flavour and become perfectly edible so you won't have to throw them away! Maybe you have found on special offer half a kilo of small, ripe tomatoes and the taste is too good to be missed, but you are worried about having too much produce to eat. Slice the tomatoes that you are not going to eat and dry them on the teflon sheet (not directly on the tray as they will stick to it, seeds and all!). After a few hours you will have delicious "sun dried" tasting tomatoes to add to your dishes such as tomato sauce, condiments and sandwiches. You can keep them dry, or frozen, or make a delicious conserve in tomato sauce if you know how to preserve food. Yummy!

Some more cool things you can do with a dehydrator are Christmas wreaths made of fruit, multi-colour fruit smoothie roll ups, raw cereal bars, breakfast cereals, edible decorations, salt and flour dough crafts etc.

Just look up on a search engine and you will find tons of websites full of recipes. The fun, the savings and the quality of food are excellent and a dehydrator is most certainly a very good appliance to create food storage for now and for an uncertain future.

14
GROWING YOUR OWN FOOD

"Gardening requires lots of water - most of it in the form of perspiration." (Lou Erickson)

I have the feeling that if everybody would grow most of his food we wouldn't be as worried about our future. Food and shelter are the two basic necessities of life. Excess produce can be stored, bartered, given away or sold. Gardening is always a positive undertaking. I hope you will feel too, that you need to grow your own food; this will improve your financial situation while increasing your well-being and inner peace.

I am not a professional gardener but every year I try my best to grow what I can and after almost ten years I can look back and see that I have learned a few things by trial and error. It would have been much easier if I had had a guide to tell me what I was doing wrong, but nobody was available then!

Nowadays there are so many TV shows, books, magazines and internet sites with gardening advice that one wonders why we are not all expertly pottering about in our gardens. Some people don't have much free time or interest, others would love to get started but don't have a clue on what to do first, so I am addressing my remarks to them. I am answering the questions that I hear every day and that I used to ask all the time.

Sometimes the available advice is far too advanced for complete beginners; jargon is used and assumptions are made, so beginners shy away. However, gardening can be very rewarding, relaxing, and good for our health as staying in the fresh air in contact with nature (that's a polite way of labelling weeds) promotes good health and good mood. Of course, let us not forget that growing our own organic food has strong economic implications - we can save money and become self-reliant. When we produce some of our food we reduce, to a certain extent, the impact of inflation on our money. Gardening is just too useful to be ignored!

Instead of mowing and watering a useless lawn twice a week and looking at a boring flat area from your windows, you can have a smaller lawn and lots of trees, shrubs, flowers and vegetables to add variety, colour and wildlife to your garden. In fact, a look at any garden makeover programme on television will prove that a garden featuring plants growing vertically, flowing little paths and crowded plants for some reasons looks much bigger, deeper and more exciting than a perfectly manicured lawn.

How can I get started?

The first thing to ask yourself is: where do I want to grow my plants? Indoors, in pots? In the conservatory? In the garden? In an allotment? In a balcony? On the flat roof of your property? Whatever your chosen area is, it must supply 6 to 8 hours a day of sunshine to the plants, unless of course you choose only shade loving plants such as ferns and spinach. But that's another topic!

Your pots, raised beds or transplanted plants want to ripen mostly in the sun, so you need to visualise in your mind at what time of the day you get the sun in that area and maximise your chances to expose the plants to the necessary light so they can thrive.

As for tools, purchase some sturdy, good quality metal tools which will last you years and years, instead of cheap and cheerful plastic toy tools which will disappoint you, and will need replacement really soon.

All you need is a pair of gloves, a little spade and some secateurs (a type of cutters), and perhaps a rake if you have a tree that every year loses masses of foliage. A hoe is also useful to do some weeding without bending too much.

If you think that every plant you touch will die, try the easiest plants on earth: potatoes and strawberries. No gardener is so unlucky as to lose these two! They are the kind of plants that you just plant, water regularly and forget all about until harvest time. Meanwhile you will be learning about general gardening while being reassured that you can successfully grow these two plants.

Which plants shall I grow? Well, the plants that you actually eat, of course! (I leave comments on ornamental gardens to specialised books; we are trying to grow food to save money here!)

What should I do now?

Let's say that you have chosen to grow peas. To grow peas you will need to buy either a bag of seeds by February, or a 5-inch tall plant by April. If you start planting just before summer, you will be too late to see the plants grow and produce fruit, in most cases. If you want to grow potatoes, buy the best looking and dirtiest potatoes from your local market, shop or supermarket. Avoid as a plague seed potatoes from garden centres as often they are sterile. This means that they are modified on purpose, so that the potatoes that grow from these seed potatoes don't have the capability to reproduce themselves. This leaves you with no option but to buy new seed potatoes every year - excellent for the owner of the garden centre, but very dear for your pockets.

What medium do I need to buy for my seeds or plants?

You need compost (soil), water and light/sunshine. You may also grow plants in hydroponic media but this is a bit specialised for the purpose of this book so I recommend you do your own research on that. You may want to grow in pots, raised beds, or directly on the soil. Any container with some holes for drainage can be used for plants - be creative! From water bottles to milk cartons and old cooking pots, everything can be recycled. In fact, a simple toilet roll centre is excellent for most seedlings and can be replanted directly into the soil where it will break down.

I have the seeds and the compost - what now?

Follow the instructions on the packet! Check that you are in the correct season for planting (lots of plants are started off in February- March), spread the seeds and cover lightly with soil, then water (don't flood!) The seeds may take from 1 to 8 weeks to sprout - always plant more then you need because sometimes not all the seeds develop into big, healthy plants. When the seed start developing little shoots, you have your new baby plants. Keep watering them as necessary and transplant them to their final place as instructed on the seed packet or on the plant information label.

What kind of compost should I use?

Usually a basic compost from a reputable garden centre is OK for most plants (but some want a different type of compost, such as Ericaceae - Heathers - which want an acidic soil.)

However, for a really special compost mix, check out this website: www.squarefootgardening.com. This website explains which is the optimal mix to grow healthy plants in raised beds. They suggest a mix of 1/3 peat moss (to hold the moisture), 1/3 vermiculite (to drain easily) and 1/3 compost (to nourish the plant). As peat is precious and not to be wasted, you can choose an alternative such as bark, wood fibre, coir, biosolids, bracken and green compost. The soil is the food of the plant and it can determine life or death so it's important to choose the correct one. To enrich a poor soil add compost, manure and live worms!

Should I plant the seeds or sprout them indoors or outdoors?

For some plants you can choose either, depending on the temperature of the soil (usually after the last frost). However, I like pampering my seeds and I always sprout them indoors, let them grow strong and tall and eventually transplant them when they are at least 10 cm tall.

This year I dared putting 20 pea plants outdoors when they were only 5 cm tall. The day after, they were had all been cut in half by some obnoxious wood pigeons! This means I have wasted weeks of work. I quickly re-planted lots of new seeds, gave them a quick start in my sunny conservatory, and transplanted them when they were much bigger.

Ten years ago, the first time ever that I tried a bit of horticulture, I planted some seeds straight in my garden. I had spent quite a lot of money for asparagus seeds and many special plants. Imagine my reaction when the morning after my hard work, I found out that some cats have dug the whole area and used it as their toilet! That put me off gardening for a couple of years - until I found out about sprouting! Novice gardeners don't need any disasters when they get started.

A word about plants that have been germinated and grown indoors, or in a garden nursery. These are tender plants, which are used to a still environment, with no wind, a constant temperature and constant watering.

When you take them outside in the real world, do so a bit at a time so they can harden. I would usually take them to the garden during the warmest time of the day in spring, and then back in each evening for a few days. Then I would put them out for 10 hours a day for a week. Finally, if the threat of frost is gone (end of April?) and the plants are looking happy, I leave them outside for a few nights to see how they are coping. If they start shrinking and dying off, I immediately bring them back indoors, feed and nourish them until strong again, and re-start the weaning process. This is usually enough to save all the plants from disaster. However, you never know what the British weather has in stock for you. In the late spring I had a long week of summer weather and I transplanted all my tomatoes and courgettes outdoors after the usual weaning process.

The sun was really hot, and the sky was blue. During the late evening, a gale force wind suddenly swept my region and in the morning I was devastated to find my plants broken in pieces, torn, and shrinking. The wind was still strong so I quickly pulled them out, repotted them and nourished them for a couple of weeks - I lost only about 20% of them. When it was the time to go out again, I planted them all with care, then I covered them with plant fleece as a protection and I only took it off during hot days. After 2 weeks, I took the fleece away for good and my plants have thanked me by growing really vigorously. I am not saying that you have to rescue all your plants in this way, but it definitely worked for me! My plants did so well, that I had a wonderful tomato crop of about 3 full bowls a day in August, September and October and my dehydrator was working day and night to preserve my special "sun-dried tomatoes".

How do I know when my plants need water?

Good question! No watering in autumn, winter and early spring unless really hot and dry. I usually water my plants at least once a day during the hot season if they are in pots as containers evaporate very quickly. Anyway, when I see that the plant leaves are dropping or wilting I know that I urgently need to water it. Usually the surface needs to be always a bit moist. However, some plants want only a little water - you need to read those seed packet instructions well! Basil for example wants frequent watering, while stevia hates having wet roots.

A good idea is to group together thirsty plants and separate them from dry-loving plants so you don't treat them all in the same way, which could result in disaster! Of course you could also invest in a water-butt and automatic irrigation system (see below).

What jobs do I have to do and when?

Look up in the BBC or RHS gardening calendar section and copy the keywords into your own calendar. For example they might say, March - weed, prepare bed, dig and plant. This means that you need to get rid of unwanted plants, prepare the soil (bed) for planting etc. In summer they might say, "August, fertilise" etc. If you quickly write a note in your calendar of the main jobs to do in every season you will eventually remember to do them year after year.

What happens if my plant has a problem?

Most times, people develop their skills after fighting a plant problem with a virus, a fungus, lack of nutrients, or an attack by little pests. If your plant looks unhealthy you need to find out what's up, and quickly! Do you have a Vegetable plant expert manual? They are invaluable for quick help. Otherwise a Google search may help. Simply type what you would ask i.e. "why my raspberries have leaf scorch?"

You will see some answers, many will be contradicting one another, but eventually you will determine what is the main issue. If you are still lost, can you ask a gardening neighbour? He might know exactly what's wrong. Sometimes plants develop a problem simply because we have forgotten to use the right fertiliser, or we are watering too much or too little, or it's too hot, too cold etc. Other times they just give up whatever we do - the important thing is to learn from our experience and try again!

I want a person to come and see my garden to help me but I have no money, what could I do?

This is a typical problem but it can be solved. First, think of any of your friends who are already doing gardening and try to see if they want to share their knowledge. Usually those who successfully grow plants are enthusiastic about the topic and they don't mind being asked questions. Second, if none of your friends can help, look in your area for gardeners' clubs and associations and see if you can join for free. Third, look on the internet for this association: http://mastergardeners.org.uk This is an association of Master Gardeners who can give you free local advice and support for a year and train you to become a Master Gardener yourself if you wish. They are dotted around England and are spreading steadily. Their website is full of news, events and advice tailored for beginners who wish to get started and enjoy the fruits of their labour.

What size of plants can I grow?

It depends on the space available. If you grow large plants such as rhubarb, courgettes, sunflowers, tomatoes or gojiberries you need a rather large area of 1-2 square metres each! Other plants such as sweetcorn need to be planted in groups of four to pollinate each other, so you can allow 1 square metre for four plants and remember that they grow very tall. Other plants such as radish and certain types of lettuce don't require a large area and are happy to grow in pots on windowsills.

Can I choose any plant I wish or are there "difficult" plants?

It depends on your experience, tenacity and how quickly you can solve arising problems. I am not an expert, but so far I have noticed that Mediterranean plants, which normally grow in really sunny and hot areas, do not perform very well outdoors. For example, this year I am growing all my sweetcorn indoors; I have four of them in a 50 cm (20 inch) wide container with three inches of soil, and they are thriving, although their cobs are maturing later than usual.

Other years I tried sweetcorn outdoors, and when summer was dry and hot I had a good harvest, but when we had cloudy summers the plants just didn't grow enough to produce any food, which was disappointing, after investing so much time and energy in them. The same goes for peppers (not chilli peppers). I tried them outdoors starting with an established plant but they shrunk in the cold British summer and died off in a month. This year I planted all of them from seed and kept them all indoors and they are still alive, growing peppers up to 5 cm long by mid August. So I assume that sun and heat-loving plants will thrive indoors or in conservatories and greenhouses. The best thing is to check what your neighbours are growing: if it's doing well in their garden it should be thriving in yours (climate wise) but do consider soil, wind, weeds etc. If the desired amount of heat is reached, the fruit will taste sweet.

I hate weeding, what shall I do?

Join the club! You can learn on the internet how to fork weeds back into the soil and use their nutrients as food for other plants. Also, if you really can't bend and pull weeds, do use the square foot gardening system on a raised bed to the height you can cope with without bending. Square foot gardening is very good for those who prefer to sit in a chair and work at a table. The perfect mix is easy to work with even after 3 or 4 years (it's not hardened clay soil with stones!) and pulling the occasional weed is easily done with two fingers (unless it's a stinging nettle, in which case it's better to use gloves!). Because people don't walk on square foot gardening containers, the soil is not compacted and it never becomes hard. However, if you leave the weeds untouched for a year, do expect them to strangle anything growing nearby with their roots and branches. Instead of pulling them one by one, use a hoe, and after cutting them fork them back into the ground as fertiliser. (But don't fork them in, if they have gone into seed or they will centuplicate!) When weeding, the best way to make sure you are removing a weed and not a valuable plant is to pull on it...

How can you tell if a plant is a weed?

Simple: apply Murphy's Law. If it grows vigorously, never suffers from any diseases, and when you pull it it's hard to get out of the ground, it's a weed. However, if it pulls out easily, has problems of all sorts and is infested by aphids, it's usually your favourite plant. If you find you have ground elder, it will be cheaper and easier to either let it grow and eat it as salad or move house - it's the most invasive weed I've ever dealt with, and it keeps coming back even after using Root Out! One of the hardest weeds to remove is Japanese Knot Weed - search on the internet for suggestions on how to remove it.

How do I know if a plant is better to be grown in a pot or container?

Apart from looking at the plant in the usual websites, as a rough idea keep in mind that you want some plants to be restricted in their growth so they don't spread and take over the whole garden. A few come to my mind: mint, comfrey, strawberries and fig trees. These are all suited for large pots where they can thrive without disturbing! But if you frequently forget to water your plants, pot plants will suffer and die - either set a reminder for your watering routine or plant those poor creatures in open soil to give them a chance to live!

I would like to make my own compost, how do I get started?

Go to websites such as www.gardenorganic.org.uk/composting for detailed advice. In brief, composting means to create your own rich and fertile soil by piling up together your raw fruit and vegetable peelings, grass cuttings, weeds, tea bags and leaves, coffee grounds, cardboard, paper, fallen leaves, hair, nail clippings, crushed egg shells etc. A full list is available in any book or website about composting. Meat, fish, cooked food and cat/dog stools are not to be composted, as they will attract vermin and rats. One good thing about composting is that you will not throw away lots of stuff in the normal bin but in your compost bin, so you will have less waste to send to landfills.

Do I have to buy a compost box?

Not really! You can make your own with wooden pallets if you wish. As long as there is a lid, no gaps and some heat during the day you can obtain as much compost as with a normal plastic bin. One word of warning though: whatever you choose, remember that compost material needs to be forked and moved at least once or twice a month, and it is really heavy to move when the container is full!

Ask a friend if you can try to mix their compost bin (I guess they will be just too pleased to allow you!) If you find out that is beyond your best effort, invest in a rotating (tumbling) compost bin. If the money is tight but you just cannot turn things in the normal compost bin, then you might want to save up for it - you are worth it and your back will be forever grateful!

A tumbler compost bin costs between £90 and £150. After a long search, I found a few on the internet. However, I hate to admit it, I think it's better to make your own. I spent hours and hours reading the customer reviews on every single compost maker that was not the traditional basic plastic bell. I read pages of descriptions of each compost tumbler, wormery, earthmaker compost bin, envirocycle composter, rota composter and so on. What I understood is that you will spend quite a lot of money for a composter but in none of the models I checked (about 50) were the customer reviews 100% positive. There was always something bad - and I am not talking about the quality of compost produced, because that depends very much by the experience of the person throwing the right things in etc. I am talking about lots of faulty machines featuring any of the issues outlined below:

✓ flimsy plastic, that bends and breaks easily

✓ lids that are extremely difficult to close, and then impossible to open without a tool of some sort

- ✓ tumbling composters that don't tumble, are too heavy to rotate and don't have enough handles

- ✓ spindles that break after 2 days

- ✓ nuts, bolts and internal parts falling into pieces from day one

- ✓ rusty legs on the metal stand for the tumbler

- ✓ low quality wood and broken pieces upon arrival

There is much more to know than that which I am quoting but I think that by now you've got the idea. If I were paying £40 for such a compost bin, I could almost accept some imperfect parts, but costing almost £200 - excuse me if I say it - then I expect a seriously good tumbling composter of sturdy quality, steady on its feet, with stable internal parts, and with handles strong enough to manage to turn the enormous weight of a full container. Well, I couldn't find one; having checked all the customer reviews I can say honestly that you will be far, far better off making your own with three pallets and some strong wire. And you don't have to believe my words: simply Google "customer review for..." (name of tumbling or normal composter) and read all the reviews. You will be surprised... I hereby invite composter producing companies to come out with a design for a composter that stands that test of time and is designed ergonomically. If you find a good one, please post a comment and link in my blog, so I can buy it!

Do I need to buy a kitchen caddy?

Possibly. A kitchen caddy is basically a small container where you can quickly put your composting bits before you get the chance to go to the garden. Usually you can buy special liners for it, made of materials that degrade naturally. If you can't afford one, you may use a small washing up bowl and keep it covered so it won't attract those tiny flies that love compost heaps. It's really useful to have one also because fresh food starts rotting a bit there, so it starts the process of decomposing before getting to the compost bin.

So, to sum up, composting works like this: Every day, when you slice fruit and veggies or use any materials that are good for composting, put them in your kitchen caddy or directly in your composter. The smaller the bits are, the faster the composting process will be. Don't throw whole banana peels, watermelon peel or whole cabbages. They will still be intact next year! The easiest way is to cut them while you cook and put them aside right away so you don't have to wash the cutting board and knife again. Some people freeze their cuttings - it helps. In winter days you might prefer not to go outside very often so you will find that the kitchen caddy becomes invaluable. Don't put your composter so far away from the house that you give up the idea of ever walking there in the cold or rain! As often as you remember, give a good mix to the compost, so that everything decays nicely. In three months there should be some good compost ready (it takes longer in winter). If nothing has happened or the compost actually stinks, you might have put the wrong ratio of dry and wet elements. Look it up in books or on the internet. Nettles and comfrey are excellent starters for composts and they give lots of fertilising materials to it. You will start looking at nettles with a smile once you know how useful they can be (plus they make a tasty nettle soup!). If the amount and balance is right, but still no compost, maybe you forgot to turn the waste! If you are desperate, open the bin, throw everything down on a large plastic sheet, give it a good mix with a fork, and with a spade put it back inside. Then proceed to order a tumbling composter! Another tip: if you find a worm when doing your normal gardening, gently pick him up and put him in the composter. Worms are a blessing as they do the entire job for you. Put as many as you can find and if you get started with a family of 500 worms, apparently they can expand to a condominium of 20,000 in a couple of years! Now, that's a quick compost maker!

How about water for cleaning equipment and to water the plants?

Plants need regular watering and this can be an added expense to a stretched budget. There's no need to worry, if you place a water-butt to collect rainwater. You spend the money once, and it should last for many years. Most water-butts come with a tap; make sure they are high enough from the ground, so you get enough pressure, or it will take you ages to fill up a watering can. One way of sorting this problem is to fill up two watering cans; while you water an area of your garden you fill up the second watering can and then you swap watering cans.

Some clever people have devised a system with a water-butt placed half meter from the ground, and surrounded by a protective bar to avoid falls. They connect an old hosepipe to the water-butt and run it around crucial areas of the garden. That hosepipe has regular holes on its surface, so that the water can come out. When watering is necessary, all that needs doing is to open the tap and let the pressure do the work. Water from these containers is not safe to drink, but may be used to wash dirty garden tools and your car, saving a good deal of money in the long run.

If you have the funds and the space, you may even want to create an old style system for washing outdoors. You need to build a structure that is strong enough to hold the water butt in an upright position a metre from the ground. Under the water-butt, place an old sink, a large type so that you can fit buckets inside it. The sink will need some worktop and waterproof structure there to stay in place. Connect the waste water with a pipe that goes to your nearest drainage area.

If designed well, you will achieve a little area where to wash dirty Wellington boots and all sorts of things that would bring mud in the house. You can also use it for filling up watering cans so they don't overflow on the ground, flooding it.

A cheaper, less stable alternative is to purchase a mobile garden sink with wheels, which comes with a central basin, plug, chain, waste pipe and draining and work surfaces. For less than £36 it is a good bargain; it folds flat and can be kept in any outbuilding until needed for a camping trip for example. I found this one under the "general garden tools" area in www.selections.com. The same company supplies useful apple, potato and vegetable storage packs for your surplus products.

Trees, berry bushes and climbing plants

A garden without trees and shrubs may look quite flat and boring. It is also a bit uninteresting and too exposed for wildlife such as birds and frogs to feel safe. If your garden is in shade the whole day, I doubt you can grow much food in there. Maybe spinach! However, there must be a sunny outside wall on your property somewhere and on that wall you can train some trees such as figs. First of all if you have already some trees and they don't produce any fruit (the reasons can be lack of pollination, early frost, disease, old tree etc.) either fix the problem or remove them and plant 2-3 year old fruit trees.

Moreover, you can grow grapevines on your South-facing wall. We bought one in 2005 and six years later it is a vigorous, 4 metre high plant, providing us with lots of grapes every autumn. We liked it so much that we bought a new grapevine every two years and now we have four at different stages of growth, all in sunny areas. Their foliage offers a hiding place for lots of useful bugs and food for birds, it's attractive and gives a nice cottage look to our uninteresting 1960's house. Our two bigger vines produce more than enough grapes for our family for a couple of months - so we don't have to spend every day around £2.00 for a punnet of grapes that has travelled all the way from a Mediterranean country.

Buying trees

If you love fruit you could consider buying some trees of appropriate type and size for your garden and climate. First, check if they need a companion tree or bees for pollinating. Failure to do so may result in pretty flowers but no produce. Second, see how much you can invest. A fruit tree in a pot costs from between £15 to £30 but it's a good long-term investment. You want to transplant that tree so that it will establish itself well. Some trees can grow in pots: figs and peaches for example. Pots must be of a minimum diameter of 50 cm (20 in), and 45 cm (18 in) deep; anything smaller will lead to trouble - it needs to be watered every other day during summer so if you are away your tree may suffer or even die.

Remember to buy a tree on a dwarf rootstock or that lovely little plant will eventually grow to several feet high and dominate the entire garden! The best time to plant these trees outdoors is the December/January period when the trees are fully dormant. A soil- based compost such as John Innes compost number 2 can be used as the growing medium.

Apples, pears and figs may be planted and trained as "espaliers". *Espalier: a fruit tree or shrub whose branches are trained to grow flat against a wall or a fence, supported on a lattice or a framework of stakes.* You don't want to use wood to support those trees as it will eventually rot. Trees growing as espaliers require extensive knowledge and understanding of the principles of fan training, so a good deal of time will be spent researching the topic with the help of websites, books or a gardener. The advantage of this investment is that you will be able to grow several types of fruit trees in a rather small area, and enjoy their product for 15 to 20 years (50 for almond trees) - not bad at all during a recession! I found some good info in Wikipedia and also in www.realenglishfruit.co.uk, under the "tree training" section.

Other trees that can be suitable for a small garden in open soil are most apples, pears, cherries apricots, plums, and nuts on dwarf rootstock. Nut trees can cost up to £55 plus delivery. You can grow almonds, walnuts and hazelnuts etc. A small bag of nuts costs around £2 so as soon as your tree is able to produce ten nuts you will have a refund of your investment. A healthy almond tree can produce between 30 and 50 pounds (14 to 23 kg) of almonds each year - sounds like you can almost start up a small business! However, plants start producing after 3 to 5 years so a bit of patience is needed.

And now, a little bit about berry bushes

Berry bushes can be used for landscaping as well as for producing food. The choice is huge, starting from blackberry, gooseberry, raspberry, to gojiberry, juniberry, barberry, currants etc. Research which type of bushes can thrive in your garden soil, and get thorn-less varieties if you are concerned about getting hurt when picking the fruit. A handful of freshly picked berries are ten times more flavourful than their shop counterpart, which has travelled a thousand miles by truck or plane before arriving in your kitchen. If you grow berries you can try to prepare some delicious home made smoothies, ice cream and preserves. You can also freeze the berries for later use. Every time you pick some berries, put them in the freezer on a plate, making sure that they don't touch each other. After a couple of hours, take them out of the freezer and put them in a bigger bag, then back to the freezer. With this simple trick, next time you wish to use them up, you will not have to use up all the contents of the bag, because they will not solidify into a big block.

Other edible plants and herbs

There are lots of edible plants that add a splash of colour in the garden and supply cheap, tasty, healthy alternatives to supermarket produce full of chemicals and plastic packaging. Look for lavender, chives, nasturtium, dill, sage, basil, onions, yarrow, fennel, mint, oregano, parsley, sage, borage and thyme.

Lots of herbs can be planted indoors, and kept on your windowsills and balconies. Ferns like the humidity of bathrooms. Be creative and swap cuttings with your friends - simply cutting a stem, and putting it in the ground until it roots can reproduce many of these plants. Sunflowers are easy to grow and produce plenty of edible seeds. If you want to grow lots of them you may want to learn how to press the seeds to make sunflower oil!

Can I plant anything when summer is over?

Just because it's almost autumn, that doesn't mean that you are finished with gardening. You can plant lettuce, spinach, turnips, radish and potatoes and harvest them in January - March (but harvest lettuce, spinach and radish every 2 weeks). Potatoes can also be planted in a large pot and kept indoors to over-winter. Cress can grow on your windowsill and probably rocket will do, too. But do remember to bring indoors any pots of non hardy plants in September: from stevia to sunflowers, anything labelled "tender" needs to return home to be safe, or you will lose the plants with the onset of colder temperatures. Some leaves will become brown and brittle and then the whole plant will become dry and die.

Can I grow plants in greenhouses and conservatories?

Of course you can. I think that in spring, when outside temperatures are decent during the day but cold in the night, a greenhouse or conservatory can help to get those tender seeds established before going out into the soil. As long as you have frosty nights, it's safer to stay indoors. However, do remember that greenhouses usually come with a tiny 12-month guarantee and their glass smashes ever so easily, leaving you with trails of sparkling and sharp shards all over the soil.

Insulation is bad in greenhouses and therefore they can still be far too cold for certain plants. A well-insulated conservatory can be used with better results for small plants. If there are double walls, double-glazing and good insulation with a temperature that doesn't fall below 12°C (54°F), I think all your plants will germinate quickly and become strong in a good conservatory. So, if you have one, you can use it as your little indoor forest!

Can I save my own seeds?

It's a very wise idea to save your own seeds. There are lots of reasons why this will be useful and save you money in the future. Seeds are already very expensive, plus we must realise that some well-known companies called by some "seven sisters" are going to be controlling the seed market worldwide, and heirloom seeds won't be able to be bought easily anymore. The companies that will control seeds are Syngenta, Dupont, Basf, Dow Agro Sciences, Monsanto, Cargill and Arthur Mills Daniels. Their strategy is clever. First they offer 6 months worth of seeds to farmers, then, they make sure that farmers can't stop buying from them (these GM seeds are sterile, and after using them no normal seed will grow anymore on that soil). If you want to know more, research the topic on the internet; the Italian economist Eugenio Benatazzo has mentioned many times the problem of patented seeds, and its impact on the availability of food on the planet. Saving seeds is a good idea also because lots of them are edible and very nutritious. For example the humble sunflower can grow taller than an average adult and gives hundreds of seeds. In the end of the season, cut down the huge stem and keep the dry seeds in tight containers for snacking and planting. It's also a cheap food for feeding birds.

How can I fight bugs and snails without chemicals?

You need to learn about companion planting. By putting together the correct plants you can increase productivity and pollination and reduce pests. Perhaps not all of them will disappear but it will make quite a difference. Even certain types of weeds such as dandelion are beneficial for the garden. There are some insects that are useful, too. Ladybirds, for example, eat aphids and therefore help to reduce the use of pesticides. Learn more by searching Wikipedia or any book on gardening.

Get your children to help in the garden

"Yes, I am positive that one of the great curatives of our evils, our maladies, social, moral, and intellectual, would be a return to the soil, a rehabilitation of the work of the fields"
(Charles Wagner)

Small children love playing with mud, sand and water, and some are enthusiastic bug and worm hunters. As soon as they can toddle, get them a kids' gardening set with tiny fork, spade and rake and let them have an area where they can mess about while you do your gardening. A tiny watering can is also fun for them, however bear in mind that they will continually ask you to refill it, and they might eventually flood your dry-loving plants if you don't establish early some rules of where the water can go.

Once your children are ready they can help with easy jobs such as gathering leaves, light weeding, collecting seeds, watering, etc. It is better to teach them to identify and not to touch toxic plants such as Fox Glove (digitalis), Deadly Nightshade (belladonna), Poison Ivy, or nettles which sting and might put them off gardening for a while.

It is wonderful to enjoy some exercise and fresh air in the garden as a family, and when your kids are about 3 years old, they can plant their very own sunflowers and tend them carefully. Teach them the miracle of life through the cycle of germination, sprouting, flowering and so on.

Show them the tiny seedlings and let them help picking them when ready. A child who grows up tending vegetable plants is much more likely to eat fruit and vegetables than his television glued peers; he has more chances to appreciate hard work and nature and less inclination to watch TV or play with video games all the time.

He will learn a valuable self-reliance skill, which might develop into a hobby or a career in the future. I hear that gardeners earn way more than shop assistants and catering assistants, so way to go in busting the recession with gardening skills.

If your child isn't too interested yet, try to involve him by looking at keywords "children gardening" on the net for resources he can use. You will find plenty of websites with colourful games, activities and worksheets to keep young minds occupied. A little explorer on a mission can enjoy his trip in the back garden wilderness armed with a magnifying glass, a worksheet to tick when he finds a special bug or plant, and a sticker waiting for him for each achievement.

One plant that my children find particularly fascinating is Dionaea (fly trap). It's a small carnivorous plant that can grow quite big and has special leaves that eat up bugs. If you touch one hair of those leaves and a second hair within 20 seconds, the leaf will close! If an insect is trapped inside, the plant will digest it within 12 days by releasing a special liquid to dissolve it. These plants love light and humidity and they need feeding one or two bugs a month - not 10 flies a day! The effort might kill the plant. Children can show quite an interest in these special plants.

Don't worry if your children are small and you think they will ruin the garden, or you will destroy their happiness by constantly asking them not to touch the plants. If you wait for them to be 10 years old to introduce them to gardening, I think that they will have developed other interests, and might prefer to go see their friends instead of pottering about with you. Also, you can separate the garden in two areas - one where they can run wild, and another one where they can learn to be gentle and kind to the plants. If you don't teach them to be respectful of plants now, you'll never be able to take them to any garden, park, or neighbour's garden, because they might annihilate any sign of life in their blissful ignorance! It is much better to train them early in life, to love and appreciate wildlife and to respect the beauty that Mother Nature has to offer.

Just as a small digression, we as a society could possibly survive if insurance companies, brokers, retail stores and computer companies closed down for a month. But if bakers, gardeners, farmers and millers closed their business for a month, what would you do? You would be very glad that you know how to grow a potato and you have the tools, the knowledge and the experience. Let's get those packets of seeds out of the shed!

15

HOW TO BE HEALTHY IN SPITE OF WHAT DOCTORS AND MEDIA TELL YOU

"Nothing will benefit human health and increase the chances for survival on Earth as much as the evolution to a vegetarian diet." (Albert Einstein)

I am not a health professional, and therefore I recommend that you carry out your own research and seek a diagnosis from a medical doctor. However, I am entitled to have an opinion on health matters and you are quite welcome to agree or disagree with my advice as you please. You will find that my statements are pretty much in tune with what Dr. Christopher taught (more on Dr. Christopher later in this chapter). I have formed my opinion through my personal experiences and study and in this chapter I will invite you to take charge of your own health so you can improve it with simple steps. We need to be more aware of how our body works, and how what we do has consequences on our health. Sometimes, even medical doctors with the best preparation and intentions leave patients to cope with chronic illnesses with no hope of improving. With all the admiration I have for science, medicine and recent discoveries, I am puzzled to see that doctors won't even ask what kind of diet is being followed when they see a patient for a health complaint.

And yet, to a great extent we are what we eat. In fact, the food we eat is used by our body to create each cell we are made of; if that food is not bringing the necessary nutrients to build up, nourish, regenerate and heal every tissue and every cell, our malnutrition will eventually cause disease to start. That's why eating junk food is the gate to malnutrition and sickness for life. One person can be obese and constantly hungry, yet malnourished at the same time - quantity doesn't make up for quality.

So, I gasp when I see for example an overweight patient, with a big stomach area, go to the doctor, here in England, for some help with a pain in his back - and he is simply told to take a Paracetamol. In our politically correct country, are doctors scared of telling the truth to patients, in case they offend somebody? If people are smoking, are eating the wrong food or doing something harmful, this will have an effect on their health and doctors should not be worried about discussing the issue with them in those precious five minutes that they allocate to each patient. That would save lots of pain, of work, of hospital appointments and of money. If the patient needs a chiropractor, a change of life-style, or surgery, he should be told.

Dr. Christopher taught that the vast majority of disease comes from constipation, a problem caused mainly by a diet based on dense or processed foods and lack of vegetable or fruit fibre, coupled with a sedentary life. Constipation (which is signalled by the lack of 2-3 bowel movements per day) means that those toxins which were meant to leave our body, are stuck inside it and cause all sort of problems. The lymphatic system and circulatory system also are affected by congestion as toxins struggle to be expelled from our organs.

You can find plenty of testimonials of people who, by switching from a junk food diet to a fresh and wholesome food diet, together with a more active life-style, have managed to recover from headaches, pains, allergies, overweight, skin problems, and even serious liver, kidney, heart and lung diseases, including cancer. And yet, I see no adverts on TV about eating fresh fruit and vegetables.

People all over the world are re-discovering the importance of eating wholesome foods and using natural medicines to heal themselves when ill. Fad diets and calorie-counting diets may work for a little while but will cause more damage than good results. But a life-long change of life style is what we need, to stop the epidemic of metabolic diseases that are shortening our lives, and making us miserable. The economic implications of metabolic disease are staggering and I don't need to quote how many million pounds the NHS (UK National Health Service) spends every year to take care of entirely preventable diseases. For this reason I shall talk about these issues in detail, in the hope that we'll all take charge of our own health and do something about it, starting with discerning between wrong advertising claims and truthful ones.

How the Media influences our health choices

Every meal or health product advertised or sold nowadays seems to be based either on chemicals or on processed foods. We are enticed to start smoking and drinking, to use addictive substances and medicines; everything is so artificial and not natural. Just how much pressure are we under to eat fresh food and to exercise, compared to the tsunami of adverts and offers for unhealthy and dangerous substances and practices? How many products are cleverly advertised as healthy, while carrying an unreadable ingredient-list that resembles a laboratory mix? Through the media we have become convinced that we need to eat certain foods in order to be healthy, and swallow a pill to instantly fix every single problem.

Prevention is certainly mentioned in some medical programs, but overall, TV adverts during any time of the day encourage people to eat crunchy, delicious, colourful and addictive pure junk. Supermarket promotions are usually on huge packages of crisps, on alcohol, on all sort of unhealthy or fattening foods. Fruit and vegetables are only discounted when they have passed their "best before" date, or with a "buy one, get one free" offer, reserved only for highly priced items. All this is making a difference to our expenditures, whether we are rich or poor.

Money can certainly buy medicines, but can't buy health and once the health is gone, life becomes much more complicated. This is especially true when we realise that with a bit of effort, we could have avoided all sorts of illnesses. In other words, preventing a problem is better than curing the disease later. And Big Pharma (pharmaceutical companies) make a lot of money by encouraging us to live unhealthily and just swallow painkillers or laxatives as needed.

Unfortunately, I witnessed the untimely death of many of my family members due to cancer. They were all eating what they thought was a perfectly balanced diet, according to what doctors and the media told them. One of my relatives was a light smoker. He always quoted scientific studies carried out by tobacco companies, showing that tobacco is not as bad for you, and smoking does not cause lung cancer. When he died of lung cancer, he wasn't so sure anymore that this was the case. Since then, I have learned that when a company produces something and then publishes a "scientific study" on its benefits, I must take their conclusion with a pinch of salt. The same principle applies to many unhealthy purchases that customers make as a result of being misguided by wrongful claims: for example sugar, meat, dairies, fried food, ready meals, tobacco and alcohol are all supported either by advertising or by retail offers.

Do our bodies need dairy products for strong bones?

Let's look for example, at one particular area where advertising and "scientifically proven" health benefits are often in conflict. I keep asking myself, "Who benefits the most from dairy products, the consumers, or perhaps the big firms that produce or distribute dairies?"

Dr. Harvey Diamond, in his best-selling book "Fit for life", states: "There is a colossal amount of information linking the consumption of dairy products to heart disease, cancer, arthritis, migraine headache, allergies, ear infections, colds, hay fever, asthma, as documented by several researchers." He then adds that milk is the most political food in America, and the dairy industry is subsidized to the tune of almost 3 billion dollars a year (in 1985).

That rings a bell even for me here in Europe. Three of my relatives who died of cancer in their fifties, were regular dairy consumers. Advertising and doctors told them that for health reasons and to keep their bones strong they needed to eat dairies every day. One of them died of stomach cancer and two of breast cancer. A few years later, a connection between cancer and dairies was scientifically made. A look at what dairies do to our body and especially to our bones will prove all the advertising we endure is just a big hoax designed to make money at our expense.

Dairies contain casein, a base of one of the strongest glues used in woodworking. There is 300 times more casein in cow's milk than in human's milk. This is because cow's milk is designed for the development of huge bones in cows. Dr. H. Diamond writes that "casein coagulates in the stomach and forms large, tough, dense, difficult-to-digest curds that are adapted to the four-stomach digestive apparatus of a cow. Once inside the human system, this thick mass of goo puts a tremendous burden on the body to somehow get rid of it. A large amount of energy is used to deal with it but some of this gooey substance hardens and adheres to the lining of the intestine and prevents the absorption of nutrients to the body. The result is lethargy and the by-products of this process leave a toxic, acid mucus in the body."

Milk is full of antibiotics, and when we ingest any dairies we are building resistance to them. Dr. William A. Ellis, a physician and surgeon, stated that "milk and milk products are a major factor in obesity and chronic fatigue." They also cause calcium to *leak* from our bones and teeth, as the coarse calcium from cow's milk is meant to feed baby cows, not adult human beings. Cows stop drinking milk after a few months and their huge bones are kept healthy by eating grass, not milk.

If dairy calcium is so important to prevent osteoporosis, why on earth are the highest number of people suffering from osteoporosis found in North America, which coincidentally is also the country that boasts the highest consumption of dairies in the world? The rate of hip fractures in the U.S. for people of many races and ethnic origins is exactly inverse to their rates of lactose intolerance. In other words, those who are likely avoiding milk as adults have the fewest fractures. Conversely, the African Bantu tribespeople consume an average of 350 mg of calcium per day (current recommendations for Americans is about 1000 mg per day) yet do not have calcium deficiency, seldom break a bone, and rarely lose a tooth. Osteoporosis among the Bantu is very rare until they migrate to the United States and begin to consume a typical, protein-laden American diet.

I wonder why my grandmother, who had plenty of meat and dairies for all her life, suffered from broken bones, osteoporosis, kidney stones and then breast cancer? Something is not right about this fad about dairies. How can you have osteoporosis and kidney stones at the same time? Breast cancer is directly connected to the consumption of dairy products. Have we forgotten how many growth hormones are injected into animals so they can reach their weight in just 6 months? Where do you think that these hormones go when you have dairies? Right inside your intestine - the centre of your immune system - and then straight in your bloodstream, to nourish cells, tissue and organs. We know that hormones are not to be taken by people with breast cancer... and yet we consume animal products filled with them. Why? Because we've been told to. Well, that's amazing.

Cow's milk and its derivatives today make up one third of the adult diet and half to two-thirds of caloric intake in children, thus replacing so much other important, nutritious food needed in the diet. This leads to insufficient intake of some important vitamins, several minerals, and healthy fibre and vegetable oils. Cancer-preventing antioxidants in foods are missing in the milk diet.

Have a look at the links section in this book and see some real figures - not the ones given by someone sitting at the Board of a Dairy company.

Excessive calcium actually causes osteoporosis, and milk won't prevent this disease. Dairy eaters suffer more hip fractures than non-dairy eaters. Dairies cause chronic congestion problems, earaches, catarrh and so on. If your children are suffering from regular ear aches and their noses seem to be always wet, try to stop dairies for a while and enjoy the results!

According to scientists, when people consume dairy products, the existing calcium in their system is used up to neutralizing the acidic effect of the dairies they are eating. If everybody is warning you that, unless you eat dairies, your teeth will fall out and your bones will collapse, well, they are wrong. They simply can't prove that. The fact is that all green leafy vegetables and all raw nuts contain calcium. Raw sesame seeds contain much more calcium than any food on earth; fruit contains calcium, especially figs, dates and prunes.

My search for a better way of achieving health

I guessed you figured out that when it comes to health, believe me, I am all for prevention - I don't care much about advertising! I've always been interested in health and medicine. But my main point isn't to focus on dairies or on any other specific type of food. Dairies were just one of the many examples of how scientific data can be manipulated, or simply ignored, to sell a product that is, in fact, not as good for us as the so-called experts try to prove. I believe that in the same way that dairies are wrongly promoted as essential or beneficial, lots of other products are promoted in the same way, from tobacco to alcohol, fizzy drinks and so on. It would be good, though, if we took charge of what we eat, drink, apply to our skin and so on. I want to make responsible choices when it comes to my own health. Because I wanted to learn more about health, I enrolled in a course at the School of Natural Healing

(Springville, Utah) and I studied until I qualified as a Family Herbalist. This is the first module of a course that leads to the qualification of Master Herbalist.

I chose that particular school because its founder, Dr. Christopher, lived an amazing life, helping others to regain their health using two simple things: a mucus-less diet (No dairies and little or no animal products!) and some herbal remedies (he created more than 50 Formulae). I read the stories of people who regained their health by eating proper, live foods while ditching junk, and I marvelled at the power, that simple herbs have, to nourish each tissue of our body down to the cellular level.

Here I was, a past believer in traditional chemical medicine, suddenly realizing that nature offers so much to restore each organ of our body to its proper function. So, I will write here a few comments that you might agree with or not, in the hope that a concept somewhere will instill in your mind the desire to know more and to take charge of your own health. This will also mean lower bills and therefore help in your financial matters.

My personal belief is that as we learn how our body works, and how to live in harmony with nature's laws, we can live a fuller, healthier life and save time, money and energy in the long run. Doctors do an awful lot of good, but we ought to take charge of our own health and do our own research, too. There are lots of types of healing practices apart from that which is promoted by your G.P., who is visited by sales people from big pharmaceutical companies, and receives some benefits from prescribing certain medicines.

A new survey from the UK Health Protection agency has revealed in November 2011 that half of patients visiting their doctor with coughs and colds expect to get an antibiotic - even though they won't help to treat viruses. And now experts have warned that over-use of these medicines has helped to create a new wave of deadly superbugs, with no new drugs on the horizon to treat them.

The British Society for Antimicrobial Therapy said that governments and the general public fail to recognise the looming crisis and there is no sense of urgency, because we are so used to getting antibiotics whenever we need them (and even when we don't need them).

In an article in the Lancet Infectious Diseases journal, professor Laura Piddock, of the School of Immunity and Infection at Birmingham University, and president of the British Society for Antimicrobial Therapy, wrote: "Antibiotics are not perceived as essential to health or the practice of medicine, despite such agents saving lives so that individuals can live for many years after infection. It will be impossible to say how many people will be affected, and whether it will be days, weeks, months or years, but it's going to happen - there will definitely be people that will get untreatable infections."

Most times there are simple, natural and healthy alternatives to chemicals, antibiotics and even surgery. For example, we have lots of hip replacement operations, which are a blessing to those whose pain is unbearable. However, if we act on prevention, we can lower the weight of an obese person, which is often a primary cause of hip pain, or work on the cause of arthritis, which sometimes is simply triggered by eating lots of acidic foods. I am simplifying things a lot here, but when it comes to the crunch, what is wiser and cheaper for a nation and the individual: to allow people to indulge in binge-drinking, and then offer them repeated taxpayer-funded liver transplants, or to teach them that alcohol will eventually lead them to a serious problem and help them to detox?

Health tips

"He who takes medicine and neglects to diet wastes the skill of his doctors." (Chinese Proverb)

I have divided this area into many sections for ease of use; however, some topics necessarily mix with others as I view the human body from a holistic point of view and not like a conglomerate of independent organs. Sometimes a problem that seems to be isolated is actually related to a specific condition in another area of the body, and without fixing the root of the problem, the secondary issue can't be solved permanently. I will only talk about some expensive health problems, but not all!

Teeth and gum health

If you think that teeth and gums are not relevant to today's issues, you might want to reconsider your views. Let's look at these Google searches for 3 key words:

- ✓ "cavities" - 15 million hits

- ✓ "gum disease" - 7 million hits

- ✓ "dentures" - 11 million hits

Perhaps this means that 50% of those with cavities will develop gum disease and 70% of the total will end up with dentures? I don't know! The fact is that in a modern, industrialised society such as ours, children, adults and elderly people alike suffer from cavities or gum disease, and a good percentage of them end up with a beautiful fake set of pearly teeth that rests in all its glory in a glass of Fixan every night.

You will find hundreds of websites and books giving you opposite advice on how to deal with your problems and you might end up with a lot of confusion, a painful mouth, and chronic gum disease. Tooth and gum problems bring stress, loss of money and wasted time through frequent visits to the dentist, which in times of financial difficulties, might be put off by some.

Although it is clear that many of us are born with inherited weaknesses, and are prone to have tooth and gum problems no matter what, this doesn't automatically mean that we have to give up the battle, and lose our teeth earlier than expected.

I hope that the information I gathered makes sense to you; for years I researched this subject thoroughly, and tried to understand why we are told to have fluoride but we still have tooth cavities, and what is the chemistry behind cavities and gum disease; I read internet forum comments and books, asked questions, and tried many different products.

I came to believe that cavities can occur when we have three conditions at the same time: a low functioning immune system, a specific type of bacteria in our mouth, and a tooth that is in regular contact with a sugar or carbohydrate. Unless all three of these conditions are present, there will be no cavities.

Another principle I learned is that those who are prone to have such problems need to learn how to clean their teeth more deeply than others. The number one priority is to do so after every single meal, then floss and use an oral irrigator. Without hygiene, we cannot eliminate those vicious bacteria that attack our tissues and our immune system is weakened by having to cope with them 24/7. Further, I learned that any cleaning agent containing SLS (Sodium Lauryl Sulphate) would actually irritate my skin and gums, so I am personally avoiding them altogether.

Why - you ask - but nobody told me! Of course, nobody in the media or industry will try to lessen their sales by telling you what sorts of chemicals are hidden in our toiletries. "Sodium Lauryl Sulphate started its career as an industrial degreasant and garage floor cleaner. When applied to human skin it has the effect of stripping off the oil layer and then irritating and eroding the skin, leaving it rough and pitted." (links are provided at the end of the chapter).

Why should you care? Because SLS is contained in shampoos, soap, cosmetics and detergents. Inform yourself! There are thousands of articles on the damages of SLS. Toothpaste containing SLS makes your gums bleed if you are prone to gum disease. I stopped using SLS based toothpaste 6 months ago. My bleeding stopped immediately. One day, just to try it, I used an SLS toothpaste and right away, my gums started to bleed again. I was struck!

There are several SLS free toothpastes for sale; I found that at my local LIDL supermarket all of them are SLS free and they cost only 49 pence! But you can also make your own toothpaste. The recipe is at the end of this section.

During my studies, I was amazed to discover that those bacteria, which cause cavities, are not present in babies' mouths. Children get them from contact with adults who put babies' dummies in their mouths before giving them back to the little ones, share cutlery, put kiddies fingers in their mouth etc. Be careful!

Everybody knows another principle but everyone ignores it: if you are prone to cavities you should not be having sweet drinks, or sucking candies and pastilles at all. I can't believe the amount of children I see with 10 or more cavities and gum disease at the tender age of 8, and between visits to the dentist they are happily chewing lollipops!

Sugar is causing their saliva to become acid and to erode the enamel of their teeth - the first condition necessary for cavities to appear. Also, most people don't realise that refined sugar lowers our immune system response by decreasing the efficiency of our white blood cells.

But any white flour, white bread, white cake, will contain a type of sugar, which is responsible of decay just as much as refined cane sugar. After eating fruit, which contains fructose, we still need to brush our teeth. Prevention is better than the cure and it saves money. Oral hygiene is so important that it needs to continue even outside of our home. If we are out and about we can carry a portable toothbrush and a small container of toothpaste in our bag. If there is no way we can use them, we might be able to carry a tiny mouthwash with us to maintain the minimum of hygiene.

In case of desperation, a chewing-gum containing xylitol (but no aspartame!) is guaranteed not to harm the teeth. In my opinion, sending the children to school with no chance to brush their teeth for seven long hours is a decision that some might regret one day in the future. When are they going to learn the habit of brushing regularly? After they have started University?

During my Herbal course studies, I learned that our diet plays an important role in the health of our body. If fresh, raw fruit and veggies, and whole-grains are not present in our daily diet, I would expect to see problems for teeth, gums, skin and all vital organs: the symptoms will be constipation, headaches, infections, obesity and more. This is because the building blocks of our body are found in fruit, veggies, nuts, and whole-grains, not in crisps, lollipops and chicken nuggets! I don't call that "food", to be honest!

I shall say no more about the subject, but will let you know that within 5 months of improving my diet and my oral hygiene, changing my toothpaste, and of using a special herbal formula designed for my teeth and gums, I was thrilled to hear my dentist pronounce my gum disease "inactive". It can be done!

Just to finish, here below is a simple recipe to make your very own, inexpensive, SLS free toothpaste. There are plenty of free recipes for natural toothpastes on the net if you don't like the taste of this one. Feel free to experiment and then let me know how you are doing!

So, to sum up, we need to achieve or introduce and maintain:

- ✓ good oral hygiene daily
- ✓ a good diet with fresh fruit, vegetables, nuts and whole-grains
- ✓ a good toothpaste with no SLS
- ✓ good condition of the immune system

About SLS:
www.health-report.co.uk/sodium_lauryl_sulphate.html

Home made toothpaste with peppermint and bark

Ingredients and tools needed:

- ✓ a mixing bowl
- ✓ a wide mouthed bottle/old moisturiser container with lid
- ✓ ¼ tsp. (1.5ml) white oak bark extract
- ✓ 5 tsp. (25ml) baking soda
- ✓ 10 or more drops peppermint extract
- ✓ 5 tsp. (25ml) vegetable glycerin

How to make the paste:

Mix the above ingredients in the bowl and stir until you reach a thick and smooth paste, adding a bit more glycerine if it needs thickening. Eliminate lumps as they may scratch your teeth instead of cleansing them. Use a spoon to pour the paste into the container. Close the lid firmly. Use the paste as if it were normal toothpaste. Your teeth will become whiter thanks to the baking soda; your breath will be freshened by the peppermint and the white oak bark will defend your mouth and gums against bacteria.

Smoking

"Smoking helps you lose weight - one lung at a time!"
(Alfred E. Neuman in the Mad Magazine)

Quitting smoking is one area that ought to be taken into account during hard times. In fact, smoking drains our finances slowly and steadily for all our life. Not only does it cost an arm and a leg, and your lungs, but it ruins your health, too. Every year in the UK 15,000 women die of smoking-related lung cancer. Dr. Max Snyder in "The Medical Aspects of Tobacco" wrote: "Cigarettes are the only substance sold that, when the user follows the instructions carefully, will result in the consumer becoming toxic, chronically ill or dead!" Even if you don't care about a smelly house, bad breath, gum disease and health problems of all sorts, simple maths proves that stopping smoking is indeed the smartest single thing one can do to save a great amount of money and re-direct it to essential expenses. I am relieved to read that 2/3 of smokers actually want to quit. If motivation is lacking, let's see the maths behind smoking, and perhaps this will help you quit for good - out of shock!

If you smoke 15 cigarettes per day for 20 years, you will spend £27,400 (assuming current prices won't increase). If you smoke 30 per day, for 30 years, you will spend £82,170. So, if a couple from the second group decides to buy a property, and they both stop smoking, they will save the beauty of at least £164,340 towards that property. That's a staggering amount of money to waste, isn't it? It trickles every day until our finances are a disaster - it literally goes up in smoke!

Nowadays, kids as young as 9 years of age already smoke. If they smoke 10 cigarettes per day for 5 years, and then 30 until they are 50 years old, do you know how much money they will have spent? £100,430. That's without adding up those cases when smoking cigarettes evolves into smoking recreational drugs, prohibited substances and then much heavier stuff, until the poor person is a drug addict and steals to fund his habit.

How many people play lottery or scratch cards in the hope to enjoy lots of money? Well, some of them could actually have that money if they simply quit smoking.

Let's say it: £100,000 would easily pay off one's University fees, a car and rental towards a flat until a job is secured. When students ask for a loan, I would like to ask them: do you smoke? And then I would re-adjust the loan accordingly, if they are proving that they haven't learned the art of saving. I know, it sounds harsh, but during a recession people might have to choose between eating and keeping their bad habits, and there is no denying that smoking is a bad habit. There are plenty of charities and websites who are willing to offer help to stop smoking now, and enjoy re-discovering the taste of food, greater health, and a more generous sum left in your bank account. You can do it!

Links of interest:

http://smokefree.nhs.uk
http://www.helpmestopsmoking.org.uk
http://www.stopsmoking.co.uk

Drinking alcohol is not as glamorous as you think

"The chief reason for drinking is the desire to behave in a certain way, and to be able to blame it on alcohol."
(Mignon McLaughlin, "The Neurotic's Notebook", 1960)

I am not going to discuss how many people harm others while drunk and then relieve themselves from any responsibility with a careless quip, such as, "But I was drunk!". Let's look instead at some figures from a report regarding drinking. Now you will say, "Wait! This book is about how to cope with hard times, so what does this have to do with the price of cheese?!"

Good question. Let me tell you why I think that alcohol has a lot to do with wasted money.

- ✓ Britons spend £30 billions on alcohol each year.

- ✓ 17 million working days are lost to hangovers and drink-related illness each year.

- ✓ Alcohol-related problems are responsible for 22,000 premature deaths each year.

- ✓ There are 1.2 million incidents of alcohol-related violence a year.

- ✓ Around 40% of A&E admissions are alcohol-related. Between midnight and 5am. that figure rises to 70%.

- ✓ Up to 1.3 million children are affected by parents with drink problems.

To top it off, so many university students find it difficult to find real friends, while their peers are out partying and getting drunk (and dropping out of courses!). If you take the time to read in some forums you will find out that this is a common complaint. Now, let's be honest with ourselves: where does the money come from to fund all of the above drinking related problems? It comes from the working population. Whoever is working sees his taxes increase yearly, to pay towards the cost of the drinking of almost the entire population. It doesn't take an accountancy genius to work out that lots of money could be saved, and health and families would be much better off, if the alcohol issue were addressed differently. The NHS is constantly reminded to allocate more funding to deal with the problem, but that funding comes from us.

We must admit that parents who drink are modelling a behaviour that their children are very likely to follow, with all the due consequences. If not for our health, we ought to curb our drinking habit for the sake of our finances and of our offspring. There are plenty of websites to help people work out how much drinking really costs to society as a whole. Next time when we are trying to figure out how we are going to fund our education, or our first property, or simply our car repairs, let us consider the binge as an "unnecessary expense," and cut it out. If you simply wish to cut down, follow this advice by Knute Rockne: *"Drink the first. Sip the second slowly. Skip the third."* Perhaps drinking makes us think that people around us are better and life is good. But the hangover later on will prove otherwise. Do you drink only to make your friends seem interesting? Perhaps it would be cheaper to change your circle of friends.

If you wish to feel full of energy you can drink fruit juices and fruit smoothies. If you want to have fun with your friends, choose some friends that are so interesting that they can be appreciated as they are - not only when others are drunk.

If you have been brainwashed by years of the media telling you that you can only be attractive and successful if you drink alcohol, then spend some time reading about the tragic life of alcoholics. When TV adverts try to convince you that alcohol helps with digestion, remember that the body needs no more help to digest than it needs to breathe: it's a natural process and if any, alcohol slows it down and makes all the food ferment.

And finally, when some clever advert will try to teach you that alcohol is good for you because it contains such and such vitamins, remember that it is the grape that contains the vitamins, not the alcohol! You can have all the goodness without the poison. Honestly, nature can do its jobs without any additions.

There is a huge industry behind alcohol and it targets you every day to convince you that drinking is good, advisable, cool, useful and even needed. Well, it isn't - it's all about making huge profits and hiding scientific studies which substantiate the damages caused by alcohol even in small quantities. Learn about the products you introduce into your body. Knowledge is power!

Statistics about alcohol, and a site to learn about drink awareness:

http://news.bbc.co.uk/1/hi/health/3121440.stm
http://www.drinkaware.co.uk

Growing food and cooking from scratch

"You are what you eat!" (Markus Rothkranz, raw food guru)

As I mentioned in a previous chapter, food, health and finances are strictly connected. If you are eating processed foods regularly, please be aware that you are paying a lot more for your food compared to those folks who cook from scratch. Your health will decline as well, as processed foods (from takeaways to fast foods, ready meals, sugary snacks, crisps etc.) simply do not supply enough nutrients to fight disease (even if they taste great!)

As your health declines, you will rely more and more on specialist advice, doctors, pills and surgery to cope with the usual problems related to malnutrition: obesity, diabetes, allergies, constipation, depression, stroke, cancer and so on. The financial cost will not be light.

Lots of people hate cooking because they can't come up with a decent meal so they have given up altogether. Cheer up! There is hope for you! Surely there is a relative, friend or neighbour who loves cooking and can share one simple recipe with you? Is it that difficult to ask for help?

There are so many cookery magazines, You Tube videos, etc., to show you step by step - from how to boil an egg all the way to complicated recipes. There are also websites on all sorts of food: Indian, Italian, raw, vegan, Kosher, dairy free, nut free, gluten free, etc.

I would suggest that you and your best friends get together sometimes for an evening of cooking together. If you are already good at it, have you taught your children how to cook? It might be an ideal time to get started. Cookery is definitely an invaluable skill when young people leave home for work, college, or to form a new family of their own. Cooking doesn't mean throwing a package in the microwave; it's about mixing different flavours, colours, scents and textures to achieve a delicious meal every time.

How about local classes? If there aren't any in your area you could organise your very own, quite informally, and swap recipes with everybody else. It can be quite fun and for some people it has led to a fulfilling full time job. (Pun intended!)

If you are fed up of the high cost of fresh food, have you considered growing your own and swapping the excess produce with fellow gardeners?

Weight loss

"Blessed are those who hunger and thirst, for they are sticking to their diets" (Author unknown)

Weight loss, diet and finances are, of course, well connected. First of all, let me tell you that I feel the deepest sympathy for those who, through no fault on their own, have a diagnosed medical condition that causes them to gain weight, even if they were to eat only lettuce for the whole day. There are also those who eat too much or the wrong type of food. And finally, there are those who for some reason, keep gaining a bit of weight, but can't put their finger on exactly what they are doing to cause such increase, as they think that they are eating healthily.

Perhaps you wish to lose some weight; I hope that my tips can be of help - I am not a trained nutritionist - so ponder my advice as one coming from a well-meaning friend and simply discard it if it is not relevant to your case. Have you tried any of the following ideas?

✓ Serve your food in smaller plates, so your eyes think "wow, full plate!" But, the serving is smaller.

✓ Eat some fruit 15 minutes before each main meal; that will give you fibre which will send a sensation of fullness to your brain, and therefore your desire to eat should decrease.

✓ If you don't manage to eat much fresh fruit, learn about smoothies on the internet and make fruit/vegetable smoothies at least once per day. Smoothies are fast, nutritious and trendy; and some catering businesses are offering them on the High Street.

✓ When you are craving a little snack in between meals, instead of reaching for crisps and chocolates, eat dates, nuts (unsalted) and sultanas. They are nutrient dense foods, which satisfy your desires for sweet or savoury things but can't be eaten in large quantities, as they tend to fill you up quickly. Although they contain a lot of calories, they actually give you essential nutrients and not empty sugars, so they are not as bad as shop-bought snacks.

✓ Don't buy anything labeled "low fat" or "diet," as they usually still contain a large amount of fat compared to meals prepared from scratch, and they use dangerous chemicals instead of sugar.

✓ Ditch fizzy drinks! They are addictive, and full of calories, sugar, sweeteners, caffeine and a host of chemicals that are not even worthy to be called "food"!

✓ If you like a fresh drink with some taste, learn how to prepare herbal teas and drink warm or cold ones. As a sweetener, choose between xylitol, molasses, honey or stevia instead of sugar. Gradually cut down until you use very little sweetener.

✓ If you regularly eat white bread, ready meals, sausages, chips, crisps, chocolate bars, cakes, biscuits, ice-creams and doughnuts, do not expect to stay thin by drinking a Diet Coke and don't expect to motivate your kids to eat radishes and tomatoes! The good news is that we can retrain our taste buds. Learn a bit about nutrition - it's a fascinating subject.

✓ If paying for gym fees is too much, you can still benefit from "exercise for free". Park far away from the school/shop where you are meant to go. Walk and bike everywhere. Use the car as little as possible. Take up gardening, walk a dog for your friend. Dance to the rhythm of your favourite CDs.

✓ Find a local friend who would like to run with you and go running together every day. It's fun and it's free!

✓ Cut down on dairy ice-cream and make your own sorbet! Simply mix in a blender your favourite fruit, put it in the freezer for 3 hours, then mix it well. Put it in again for a couple of hours and mix thoroughly before putting it back to the freezer. When the whole compost looks like an ice cream, it's ready to enjoy, with little calories, plenty of nutrients, and no sense of guilt! Variations include adding soy milk, almond milk or a base of frozen sliced bananas.

✓ Make your own ice-lollies instead of buying the sugary, chemical-laden ones from local supermarkets. You can buy the moulds in any shop/supermarket; fill with fruit smoothies or juice, leave them to set and enjoy. Children and adults love them, and you can preserve the taste of your favourite summer fruits for months.

✓ Learn how to make your own white sauce, tomato sauce, etc. Not only are they much cheaper than shop-bought ones, but also they are tastier and healthier. There are plenty of free recipes on the internet and in libraries.

✓ Don't buy, or store in your cupboards any tempting foods that you know are not good for you. Instead, prepare every day a fruit salad and a vegetable salad dressed with olive oil and seeds, and when you are hungry, grab a bit of that salad or some nuts/sultanas. Olive oil is a good type of fat for you.

✓ If any well-meaning person gives you as a gift some unhealthy food, say thank you, and then instead of putting it in your mouth or in your kitchen, give it to a good friend who is not on a diet and can cope with it. Chances are, you wouldn't be stopping after one biscuit - so it's easier to forget about them altogether!

Sport, fitness and general well being

"The part can never be well unless the whole is well." (Plato)

Those who can go to the gym, or participate in sport training, are very fortunate indeed. Others don't have the time or the funds for gym fees, but there's no need to fear: with a little bit of creativity we can think outside of the box, and still be supple and fit. Our grandparents - and those before them - never set a foot in a gym, but apparently they were more robust than we are! Maybe it was because they didn't have so many "time saving" devices!

Let me sum up what I gathered about the topic and you are welcome to pick and choose what you think might work for you. Being fit doesn't have to cost an arm and a leg.

A good night sleep

A good morning starts the night before! If you can, go to bed early (well before midnight) and wake up early, (max 7:30) following the natural rhythm of the body cycles. This will improve your performance much more than coffee, pills and "energy drinks". You will also notice that by avoiding alcohol, you will wake up with no hangover headache - plus, you will actually remember what happened last night! If you have small babies and can't sleep during the night, don't worry about my advice, they will grow up and let you sleep for the whole night, eventually!

An active morning

In the morning, as soon as you wake up, instead of staggering out of bed, have a nice stretch first. You know, like the one that cats do when they wake up. Bend gently on yourself, try to grab your toes or wiggle them if they seem too distant, or maybe just touch your knees, warm up gently every muscle and for a couple of minutes just feel your body being alive.

When you have breakfast, try to balance some complex carbohydrates and some proteins and fibres, instead of heavy and fattening sugars and dairies. Your energy levels will stay stable and you will feel more bouncy.

Cycle and walk everywhere you can

The school run can surely be done with a car if you live miles away from your target, have important appointments right after 8:30, have several kids to drop at 3 different schools etc. Otherwise, try to take the opportunity to walk or cycle to school with your children. This is a good chance to be fit and enjoy some fresh air. After cycling to school, you will feel quite hot for at least 20 minutes and you won't need to turn on the heating right away - save on your bills! Heat up from within!

Cycle and walk everywhere as much as possible. Your aerobic capabilities will increase, your mood will improve, your overall fitness will be great, your muscles will tone up, and you won't spend money for parking, fuel, fitness instructors and cellulitis creams.

If your kids are too small and can't cycle with you for the school run, shopping, etc., and if you have a good budget, invest in a cargo bike (a bike or trike with a box). Other European nationals use bikes every day until they are past 80 years of age - drivers just get used to them. I bought a cargo bike and I found it really useful for all sorts of things, as long as I am not in a great rush, of course.

Mine is a Christiania trike and I bought it in London for Christmas. www.velorution.biz/shop/category/bikes/christiania. We like it so much that I have since trained to become a local agent for Christiania! You can fit up to 4 kids in my model, or 2 adults, and the box is great for shopping and business. There are over 100 Christiania bikes in London and 45,000 in Copenhagen! Cargo bikes are fun, easy to use, and with them you burn calories, not fuel: a great way to keep fit and be green.

You can find plenty of cargo bikes with a search on the internet: just google these names: Nihola, Babboe, Winther kangaroo, Bella Bike, Trio Bike, Taga, Zigo, Christiania bikes. Try several and choose the one that suits you most. There are interest-free loans available for Christiania bikes, so it's an affordable investment in foot-power energy!

My bike insurance covers me from any problems just like car insurance would. And with fuel prices raising constantly, a bike, trike or cargo are looking more and more tempting for short trips. If you have no children and no trips to your town centre for shopping, you might want to run or cycle for charities: great motivation will support you and your fitness will improve. It's almost impossible not to smile when you are on a bike!

You can become fit at home

Nobody says that you can't be fit if you just stay at home! Dance and simple exercises can easily be done in your largest room with any music or DVD you like. Whether you do it alone or with friends it's entirely up to you; your stamina will increase and your mood too, as exercise stimulates the areas of the brain that are connected with happiness and pleasure.

- ✓ Some mothers pay around £3 or more per session to take their children to dance lessons; children can still dance and move around at home if finances don't allow anything fancy.

- ✓ Staying in the garden is bound to help you being fit: playing Badminton, trampoline, basketball, ball games, climbing trees and climbing frames are not just for kids!

- ✓ Gardening is also a great way to keep fit and improve our muscles, fighting the onset of osteoporosis. If you are not sure that gardening helps being strong, tell me, have you tried mixing the compost heap recently? Well...

- ✓ Weight lifting at the gym is a wonderful thing to do, I am sure, however dumbbells are cheap enough and food cans are even cheaper and still meet the target of lifting a weight and helping us feel stronger. You don't even need a leotard if you lift a can of peas at home! See how much you can save?

- ✓ Ask your friends if they would like to join you for a walk or run somewhere, or go to a skate park with your children and while they skate, you can play ball games with your friends.

Planning meals to maintain fitness

When you plan your meals, always include foods that will nourish you and release energy constantly instead of keeping the levels oscillating up and down. Fruit and vegetable smoothies are excellent especially for summer; hearty vegetable soups with wholemeal bread will give you cheap but nutritious meals, which are ideal in those cold winter evenings.

Do I need to specify which foods are not going to give you energy, a fresh mind, and good moods? Ready meals, takeaways, fried food, processed food, shop-bought snacks, cakes, biscuits, crisps, lollies and so on are not going to do anything good to you in the long run. Choose live food as near as possible to its natural state and your body will thank you with renewed energy, a sharper mind, good moods and a general increase in health. I wouldn't go for a 100% raw food diet, but it seems that a balance of at least 60% raw food, including fruit and nuts, complemented by cooked or sprouted beans and whole-grains, can really give most people the health and energy they are looking for.

There are several meal planners available for free on the internet and with some effort you can accomplish a good result. Start by having a complete day every week with only health-boosting foods and then increase the number of days you eat healthily.

Chances are that, as your energy increases, your weight decreases and little pains disappear, you will enjoy it so much that it won't be a difficult task to ditch most or all of the so called "junk foods".

16
HOW TO HAVE A GOOD TIME WITHOUT SPENDING A FORTUNE

"Attitude is a little thing that makes a big difference."
(Winston Churchill)

There might be a point when some of us will wonder if having cable TV or Sky, eating at restaurants or attending parties and baby/wedding showers is a bit too costly for our budget. However, I wouldn't be so negative: people can have fun with simple things that don't cost the earth. Let me jot down some ideas for you, and see if there is anything appealing to you!

If your TV subscription is costing you the earth, you are doing well in getting rid of it. It will munch away several hundred pounds a year and it is certainly not an investment. Ask yourself why do you rely on it so much and what else can you do instead of watching TV.

A regular trip to the local cinema can be great fun, but once you add the average cost of fuel (£2), the tickets (£5-£10 each), the inevitable pop corn (£2) and maybe a quick drink (£2) or ready meal in the end (£6), your budget might be stretched to the limit.

A much cheaper alternative is to gather a couple of your friends or relatives and watch a rented movie at home. Libraries rent movies quite cheaply and there are always new titles to choose from. Popcorn is very cheap if you buy the popping corn in the whole foods department of your local store: the average price is 95 pence for ½ kg, so about 20 pence per serving.

Pop the corn in hot oil and then bring the container to your friends and enjoy! Your drinks don't need to be expensive either: still water with plenty of ice and a drizzle of lemon or flavourings can be as exciting as more expensive drinks but will leave you in control of the situation!

Childrens' birthday parties are becoming so complicated and expensive that soon people will need a loan to be able to afford one. Nowadays everybody feels that they have to invite lots of friends using fancy themed paper, feed everyone with mountains of fancy foods (mostly sweets), have perhaps a professional organiser, choose a theme (pirates, princess etc.), buy theme banners, balloons, plates and table accessories, and of course give to every guest a bag of goodies to take home.

On top of this I saw chocolate fountains, fancy dress requests, bouncy castles, face painting and packages offered by leisure centres where they do all the catering for you and you pay a sum for each guest. Perhaps this is great and the child will feel special, but how is he going to feel if next year you can't afford all that, after he got used to Disneyland for the past 5 years? How will he feel if you can no longer compete with his friends' parties, so full of goodies and so fashionable?

In times like this, when the economy is certainly not looking like it's going to improve soon, it is very wise to calm down and reconsider what a birthday party really is about. To decrease the expense there are lots of things one can do:

Invite 4 or 5 people, not the entire school or office!!! Use plain paper for cutlery, drinking glasses etc. but decorate it with acrylic paints the week before in areas where food and drink won't be an issue. There are plenty of ideas on the net. Choose a theme if you really have to, but have your children use their imagination, skills and time to make their own decorations. Bake your own cakes instead of buying ready ones. Having tried several supermarket brands myself, I can reassure you that nothing processed compares to a beautiful, fluffy, freshly baked cake with 4 ingredients: water, sugar, wholemeal flour and eggs. Supermarket cakes look absolutely wonderful but are laden with chemicals of all sorts, hidden fats and sugars, eggs well past the expiry date, and with a plasticky taste. Refined sugar can be substituted with molasses, honey, stevia or xylitol, and even with fruit juice for a healthier alternative. As an alternative, find a local baker who can produce a good, wholesome cake for you for a decent price. Plain popcorn fills you up quickly and it's one of the healthiest snacks in the world!

On the net there are hundred of free games for children to do: print a couple of sheets and follow the instructions. Miming games where people have to guess something are always fun. Instead of giving to the guests a bag of cheap and cheerful plasticky toys made in China, give them a hand written thank you note, made by your children. Add a wrapped sweet or chocolate, or a cute pencil, without going overboard. Or, prepare some small bunches of flowers and leaves, put together of course by your kids.

Another option is to take a photo of everybody and print it on photo paper, and use that as a thank you note. In one year, nobody will remember what they ate or which goodies they received, but some might still keep the photo and the memories attached.

Magazines and entertainment

"I had the blues because I had no shoes until upon the street, I met a man who had no feet." (Ancient Persian Saying)

Buying lots of "stuff" is not going to make us truly happy, right? And, to have fun it is not mandatory to spend money. Actually, quite the contrary. If your account is in red and prospects are not good, you could consider cutting magazine subscriptions and organise swaps with friends' magazines instead, or using the libraries. You can even have an afternoon spent with your friends, chatting and reading magazines together after pooling your resources.

There are plenty of things that people can do to feel happy: chatting, a walk to the park, cycling, a cooking evening with your friends or kids, a special meal with your other half while the kids act like waiters, concerts in the local community, festivals, picnics in the back garden, board games, crafts, simple sports, general hobbies and dancing or singing are just some of the hundreds of things that we can do to enjoy ourselves.

For those who want to find a bit more purpose in their life, I would suggest also trying service projects to help others and volunteering; there is always somebody who is worse off than us, and giving a hand helps us to put things in perspective.

If you are stuck at home for any reason, and can't do any of the above for lack of mobility, you could write a blog, centred on a theme and join in the discussion with fellow enthusiasts about your favourite subject.

Entertainment and active learning for younger people

"It is easier to build strong children than to repair broken men." *(Frederick Douglass)*

Marvellous toys nowadays surround some children; their bedroom looks like Disneyland, but they are still bored to death. Some of them will grow to become a bit greedy and never grateful, looking for instant gratification but never quite satisfied.

In some marginal cases, this can lead to an extreme attachment to easy money and material possessions rather than to people and relationships, or even degenerate into criminality to feed an everlasting longing for what one cannot afford.

Whatever the case, recession times remind us to focus on what is important and to change our attitude: instead of trying our best to get what we appreciate, we can try our best to appreciate what we've got.

This means that the gifts we give and received should do more than just entertain us, but educate us, inspire us and build our character. Then the money will be invested instead of just spent or wasted. To me, toys and activities should stimulate imagination, creativity and role-play, as opposed to promoting aggressiveness, greed and addiction. Stories and TV programmes, DVDs and games should promote good values and good moral choices instead of denigrating them.

What we like doing as children - and what we see our parents do - often carries on as an important hobby in our life. I learned hard work and many skills from simply observing my parents doing things. I didn't spend my childhood in front of the TV; instead I made clothes for my dolls, built palaces with Lego, played in the countryside and embroidered sequins on my espadrilles shoes. I still enjoy learning and doing lots of different things. Guess what: I am never bored! There is always something to do for me.

I marvel at those people who wander around bored to death, either smashing things or looking for artificial replacements of happiness in alcohol, drugs, crime, and easy sex. How can they be so bored? There is so much we can do to improve our surroundings and to fill a day by doing good. It's our attitude that counts, not our money. The same principle applies to children and adults alike. But then, our clever, Government-led, Health and Safety Officers have made sure that when our children do go out they simply can't do anything right: in all the open spaces I see a clear sign indicating "No ball games" or "No cycling" and "No skating". And then we wonder why bored people end up smashing up everything? Well, it seems that every single game is prohibited!

✓ A toddler can have fun for hours with a simple, empty carton box. He will climb in an out of it, place his cuddly toys inside it, maybe cover them with a blanket and even join his Teddies and pretend to sleep. Or he can pretend that the box is a car or a train and make all sorts of noises while he carries his imaginary passengers.

✓ When my son was 2, and we needed him to sit quietly with us for an hour, we gave him some "blu-tac" and about 50 colour photographs carefully cut out from an old Argos catalogue. He carefully picked each photograph and placed it on the back of the chairs using the blue tack. He enjoyed himself for well over an hour, we enjoyed the peace and calm that came with it! We used blu-tac and photos for a couple of years when out and about and now our little daughter is enjoying the same activity, along with other inexpensive ones.

✓ Dressing up with adults' clothes is another inexpensive game that most children enjoy. Just pick your oldest clothes (those that have been hanging in your cupboard since the 70s or 80s and you didn't have the courage to throw away) and let your children put on what they want. Keep your camera ready! The overall effect might be quite cute and you will have some precious memories for your family scrapbook.

✓ During summer, a sand pit should keep the children occupied for hours; the sand can be kept in sealed bags until the good season returns.

✓ Cutting up images from cereal boxes and use them for craft or games is also quite popular among children. Leaf collections and flower pressing are also fun, together with paper-making.

✓ For slightly older children there are lots of word games that can be done. One of them consists in making a list of favourite subjects (singers, animals, towns, foods etc.) on a piece of paper and draw lines to form a column under each category. From two to 10 people can enjoy such a game together in teams. One person chooses a letter of the alphabet and then everybody has to write a name of a singer, animal, town etc. starting with that letter. The person who wrote the most names wins this round. You can also do this game using a foreign language!

✓ Karaoke is also very fun and can be done with any number of participants - choose any song among pop, rock, Christmas and kids' ones and enjoy!

✓ The internet has plenty of games ideas and crafty ideas to discover; children might also enjoy learning games with flash cards and computer programs. Many websites of well-known Museums offer plenty of interactive games connected to the national curriculum.

✓ Children up to age 10 will enjoy many visual, educational and musical games on the internet at http://www.poissonrouge.com and 7-14 year olds will really have fun with http://www.show.me.uk where art, science and history are presented with the aid of interactive Flash movies. Finally, for those who love maths, http://uk.ixl.com provides practice and awards for students from Reception to Year 9 (ages 4-13).

I honestly believe that there is no need to be stuck in front of the television or computer for the whole afternoon, and that children will become more proactive if they are left to find something creative to do with certain tools instead of looking at toys that do the whole of the entertaining by themselves. Lots of money can be saved, by not continuously buying new toys, and by using what we have with creativity, or by swapping toys with others. If any youngster needs to have a mobile phone, let him have it, at his own expense of course, and let him pay for all the associated expenses to develop a responsible attitude.

17
THE CONCEPT OF SELF-RELIANCE

"Industry, thrift and self-control are not sought because they create wealth, but because they create character." *(Calvin Coolidge)*

The topic of self-reliance is so vast and complex that even dividing it into several levels, and sections, you could fill books upon books and just scratch the surface. I am introducing some aspects of it in the hope to encourage you to re-discover self reliance not as a big one-off event but as a daily process to achieve independence.

Self-reliance is the capacity to rely on one's own capabilities, and to manage one's own affairs. It's opposite to being dependent on others and on their work, money or time to get things accomplished. Sometimes we become so ill that we lose some of our self reliance for seemingly easy tasks; other times we grow up in a system that encourages us to live on social benefits even if we are fit to work and live a normal life. Then there are times when we are fit to work and willing to do anything but there are simply no jobs available. Whatever the situation we are in, it is possible to work towards achieving a certain degree of self-reliance with determination while enriching our life and helping others.

Learning from history

In a not too distant past in Europe and the US, during the Great Depression and the terrible years that followed it - maybe up to the early fifties - most people were self reliant or working towards this goal. Families lived in rather modest, cold homes, often self built by the owners; they grew most of their food and even kept some animals. Mother would cook from scratch, mend everything and sew clothes for the whole family. She would also prepare some traditional herbal remedies for common ailments and work to clean richer people's houses to earn some money. Father would work long hours and the children would start early helping with chores, then helping on the farm or as an apprentice, and only a handful went on to study to University level.

Although nobody wishes to return to the poverty and ignorance that sometimes came with that package, I hear many voices asking for a return to a simpler life, based mostly on work, not mostly on entertainment and entitlement, and founded on simple joys such as family relationships rather then nightclubs and shopping.

The problems of today's fast paced world

It is not a secret that the moral tissue of this society is slowly disintegrating and giving less and less stable values to our youth. Too many children grow up without a concept of family life and true friendships. Addictions such as smoking, drinking, drugs or underage sex are now becoming the norm.

Other youngsters are free of the above addictions but grow up with the amusing concept that the Government and society somehow owe them money and have to keep them fed, give them a free house and money and look after their children while they don't even look for work. However, what one person receives without working for, another person must work for without receiving, as the government cannot give anything to anybody that the government does not first take from somebody else. As much as I like Robin Hood, it's not fair to work so that the lazy doesn't have to.

When half of the people get the idea that they do not have to work because the other half is going to take care of them, and when the other half gets the idea that it does no good to work because somebody else is going to get what they work for, that my dear friends, is the beginning of the end of any nation.

While luckily the above situation does not represent 100% of the population, its impact is forcefully felt on society as a whole. For example, taxes help both those who are ill and those who pretend to be ill. They also pay for caring for many fatherless children - whatever is the reason for their mothers to be alone. But you cannot multiply wealth by dividing it. The list of financially draining aspects is much longer than this, and the bottom line is that only as long as a large percentage of people are employed, the welfare state is able somehow to spend money on those who are in need, through the tax system. However, it is worth noting that we are in the beginning, not in the end, of a serious recession. All the major economies worldwide are shaking and stock markets are volatile. A sure sign that investors fear the future is the high increase in the price of gold, which is seen as a commodity to store for "times of need" where everything else has stalled.

Employers are laying-off workers every day and not requesting new employees, wages are pretty much frozen while prices of basic food and supplies, including oil, have sharply increased over the last five years.

Ten years ago I would buy a top quality loaf of bread for about 35-50 pence. Now £1.35 will only just do. That's almost three times more expensive than in the last decade - but my wages haven't gone up three times - I wish they had!

The fuel (petrol) price was 80 pence a litre in 2005, now (2011) it's about £1.36 per litre. No wonder why life is expensive: most of our goods travel a lot before arriving to our home, and the UK imports 75% of its fruit and vegetables. We have stopped learning how to make and repair things and we delegate everything we need to do to others so we can earn degrees and work in a specialised field. Somebody prepares our food, others the medicines, others the clothes, and so on. If production stops, how many people can grow and cook their own food, make their clothes, repair things and survive? Very few - and that is a major problem. We are just not self-sufficient as a nation.

So, to sum up, there is plenty to be concerned about when we consider that on top of it we are an aging nation with less buying power and more people to support, while the Government is in deep debt and average citizens can't make ends meet. Problems will arise even for the millions who have saved and worked for all their life.

The worldwide situation

"The art of living lies less in eliminating our troubles than in growing with them." (Bernard M. Baruch)

We live in a global society, where everybody is connected via internet and other media. An event that happens in Timbuktu has an impact in the Western world. So, one day you wake up, and find out that the price of oil has risen again because there was some turmoil in an Arab country miles away from your country. When something negative happens, the markets collapse temporarily, until investors work out how serious the situation is and adjust their goals.

Wise people have been observing for years the worldwide trends, and have been drawing their own conclusions about what will happen at home. Let's have a quick look: energy bills are rising on average 20-30% per year. Disasters, heat waves, hail storms and droughts in major exporting countries have caused the price of basic commodities such as wheat, rice, sugar etc. to skyrocket. This means that food and life in general cost more and more, while employment is becoming scarce, and people are spending less money on the High Street, because there simply isn't enough money going around.

Incredibly, the Government keeps raising fuel tax and lots of other little taxes and has cut the spending by cutting funding to lots of vital charities and businesses. However, when people spend less money, the consequence is that retailers lose business and suppliers go bust; we have seen many well-known brands disappearing almost overnight. Moreover, large amounts of people are drowning in debt, and can no longer spend money to help retailers, because they can't even get a new credit card to add to their pile of debt.

These are just two or three points that anyone can pick up from listening to the news, reading internet commentaries, and asking around how things are going. If you are unsure whether a recession is coming or not or just wish to know more, just type "recession" in Google, and you will get 112 million results! Recession seems to be a hot conversation topic - ever wondered why? For those who are prepared for it, it will be a painful but growing experience. For others who haven't prepared, there will be a tough life ahead, with fewer choices available.

What should we expect next?

"Prosperity is a great teacher; adversity is a greater."
(William Hazlitt)

It doesn't take a rocket scientist to work out that as trends worsen, taxes rise and the economy shrinks, less money arrives in the pockets of the Government, which in turn cuts more funding. Security and health related agencies have received painful cuts in recent days. I don't think a decade will pass before finding work will be extremely difficult and benefit payments will have to be shrunken to a minimum or stopped completely to avoid our country facing bankruptcy. In fact, while in the past we used to produce our own goods on national soil, plus we had government-owned transport system, Post Offices, energy supply system etc., now we buy lots of Chinese imports and have sold our good Government owned companies to third parties.

These enterprises have an eye for profit and no interest in their customers or in the nation's welfare. In fact some of them have even moved their customer services centres abroad to remain competitive - another blow to our economy and a hard time trying to talk to somebody who is not down the road but thousands of miles away.

Our salaries are devalued every day by the above situation and the less we earn, the less tax we pay. So our Government will have to tighten up the belt as the income from the taxpayer shrinks. This is without counting the amount of skilled expats who have moved to work or retire in Australia, Canada and other cheaper or sunnier countries, thus moving their financial capital and skills abroad.

The Office of National Statistics stated that the UK public sector net debt was £920.9 billion on July 18th, 2011. To this we need to add the cost of National debt, which is the interest the government has to pay on the bonds and gilts it sells. In the first six months of 2010, the debt interest payments were £21.6 billion, suggesting an annual cost of around £43 billion (3% of GDP). How long can we keep spending the money we don't have before we are bust? Perhaps another country will go bust before us and we'll follow overnight - it has happened before. We are all connected. According to rumours, the economies of Greece, Spain, Ireland and Italy will collapse just before we do as the Eurozone crumbles.

Meanwhile, many are dumping Euros and buying silver coins or other currencies, while Italian economist Eugenio Benatazzo forecasts the annihilation of the Euro and the return of the sovereign currencies in each country. Could this be possible? At the moment the stark reality is a general lack of funds to repay debts.

When there isn't enough money around, governments can "print" new money digitally. However, as this money is not backed by a gold reserve or anything of value, high inflation or hyperinflation will eventually follow. A typical example from post-war history is prices increasing 10% a day every day until basic commodities cost a thousand times more, while other goods completely lose their value. Remember when, in post-war Germany, a wheelbarrow load of banknotes was necessary to buy a loaf of bread? The way things are going, our situation won't be much different from that. But now we'll have to lower our expectations while lots of people will "expect" free housing, money etc. with no effort on their part.

Who will survive the coming depression?

"The only thing that overcomes hard luck is hard work."
(Harry Golden)

Whatever the reasons are for the terrible mess we are in, there is the strong possibility that, at some point, we will find out that money has not much value, nobody can afford to buy properties, cash is king, bartering is back, food and commodities will be sold at stellar prices, and hunger no longer just belongs to dusty history books.

The Great Depression, compared to our future economy crash, might look like a picnic in the park. This is because we won't be dealing just with something similar to the aftermath of World War II, but with national and personal debt of millions of people, added to the problems outlined above and others (welfare state, bankers and corporate greediness etc.). Do you really think that our Government will step in and save us all? I don't!

In case of doubt, there are literally thousands of books, websites, seminars and groups of people out there, who actively study the forthcoming depression, and discuss how to survive it - I didn't just wake up this morning and decided to forecast the future. Yet, there are many who want to ignore what's happening in front of their eyes.

I wondered who would survive this situation, and my uneducated guess it that it will be those who have carefully prepared for it, and are ready to work and sacrifice. A bit like in the "Ant and the grasshopper" story, there are some people who are just living with no care for tomorrow, over-spending, having fun etc., and there are others who are saving, learning skills, investing and preparing to live in a very different, down to earth, humbler way.

We are all going to be poorer, and will have to sacrifice many things we now take for granted - let's get used to the idea now. However, being poorer doesn't automatically mean "being unhappy". What really counts is not what happens to us, but what we do about it, and our attitude.

When the full weight of the depression will hit, let us remember the thoughtful words of Ann Frank in "The Diary of a Young Girl". She wrote, *"I don't think of all the misery but of the beauty that still remains"*. Attitude can have a great impact in our difficult lives. In fact, dare I say that our attitude determines our happiness, whatever our circumstances may be. During an economical crisis, our riches will not consist of the extent of our possessions, but in the fewness of our wants. As a consequence, those who are happy with the simple pleasures of life will be far happier than others, who are constantly trying to amass more "stuff" and "having a good time" at the expense of others.

What will happen to those who haven't worked for years?

Two of the many aspects of a depression will be lack of jobs and lack of money to fund our wasteful welfare system. That alone can spark a lot of problems, without even considering all the other elements such as lack of skills for many fundamental professions.

I am a bit worried - I wonder what will happen, when the weekly cheque will fail to fall on the doormat of those who haven't been employed for years. Some will be those who searched for jobs and couldn't find any, others will be those whose health problems prohibited even lifting an arm, and a third group will be of some who could have worked, but wouldn't work, "cos it's not worth the effort, innit?"

Can you imagine what will happen when suddenly these people's lifestyles will be restricted? Who will pay for the little extra that they have enjoyed, even if they were perfectly fit for work? If you think that the riots and looting we have seen in August 2011 are dead for good, think again. They are just dormant - an explosive device with a timer where nobody knows when the time is over. And that timer will go off again, when a hoard of people who are convinced that everybody owes them money, suddenly realises that the purse strings are now tight.

It's as simple as that. People of all sorts, who have in common a craving for money and goods that they can't afford right now, and a feeling of envy for those who can, may spell a lot of trouble. Some of us think that money, not work, gives happiness and success, and aim to achieve wealth and goods as quickly as possible. Others believe otherwise, and invest time and energy in learning a good trade and working hard. The latter attitude will pay its dividends during recession times. The first type will encounter several problems. Of course, we have taught to our citizens that they are "entitled" to benefits, and the benefit culture is caused first and foremost by a rather shortsighted socialist attitude to welfare. Our laws have generated a lack of interest in rising above a certain level, as it would mean losing benefits and paying taxes - God forbid! The impact on peoples character is evident. As much as one tries, he can't improvise overnight any of those skills, or the experiences and the thrifty life of those who worked hard for all their lives, and have learned step by step how to earn dignity and independence.

Which problems could affect my life?

When benefits will be drastically cut because the Government has no money left, I expect serious problems to develop. Some people will go and protest somewhere. Others will desperately knock on our doors asking for help. A third group will be less civil, and will force our doors and windows to grab their help.

I imagine that there will be more criminality, more looting, more unrest in general, and that in cities, going out at night will be more dangerous for lonely people. I imagine gangs and solitary people looking for easy targets. I am not sure if our brilliant Police Force could cope with daily looting and burglary on a large scale.

There will never be enough Police to deal with every crime on time; the prisons are already full now, and the Government has just cut off more funding from the Police, who are already so full of paperwork, that they can hardly make it to the streets.

As crime levels increase, normal citizens will obviously become worried about becoming a target and losing their property, their food and their lives. But in this clever country, if you harm a burglar, *you* get sent to prison for "assault causing bodily harm", while the burglar himself might be sentenced to stay maybe one year behind bars, and will maybe be left out a few months earlier for good conduct (or to ease prison overcrowding). Not only that, but the criminal also dares asking for damages, as if he hadn't been the one who got into trouble. If you went to a Zoo and entered the lion's cage, and got seriously hurt as a result, could you take the Zoo managers and the lion to court? No, you should have stayed out of that cage in the first place. The famous case of Norfolk farmer Tony Martin, who, after being burgled ten times, at the 11th attempt shot and killed one of the two burglars and then spent many years behind bars, stands as a stark warning to all of us.

If criminality will increase, there will be a really awkward situation: the only people with guns will be the criminals and some Policemen, while citizens will be defenceless. Guess who wins? Americans have been commenting on this aspect of our society for years.

At some point, some people will say, "enough is enough" and will get armed or fabricate their own primitive weapons for reasonable self-defence, from knives to rolling pins. There is no real freedom or justice in a country where anybody can hurt you or steal from you, and you are not allowed to defend yourself, for fear of ending up in prison.

I leave you to imagine the implications of the above situation for your life, your property and the lives of your loved ones. Although I dearly hope that such an event will never happen, I believe that a serious crisis with thousands of jobless people and increased criminality is very possible and people who get ready for it will not suffer as much as others.

Of course, if you think that the economy is going to recover brilliantly this year, the cost of living will stop increasing, and just being positive will magically wipe away any problems, you are welcome to keep your optimistic opinion. You don't even need to read the rest of this book and prepare for the future - just enjoy your life and good luck to you, my friend!

I wish you all the best! As for the others... please read on to the next paragraph.

The solution: developing self-reliance

"When written in Chinese the word "crisis" is composed of two characters - one represents danger and the other represents opportunity." (John F. Kennedy, address, 12 April 1959)

Each crisis in our life, whether personal or national, brings out the best or the worst in all people involved. One way to survive during a crisis is to plan ahead, stay positive and prepare ahead for the situation that is more likely to occur in our own area. Let me give you an example.

On the 8th of September 2005, a fuel strike started off in the UK, and went on until September 14th, 2005. The tax on petrol was already 80% and the price was a staggering 80 pence per litre, (which we would love to have now).

The strike started up as a small event, but quickly ground the entire country to a halt. Nurses couldn't go to hospital, people couldn't go to work or school, trucks couldn't do their deliveries, supermarkets were rationing goods, due to panic buying, and some people were just about to finish their food supplies and medicines.

My husband and I hardly noticed the crisis. We were actually quite amused at the amount of panic-buying that left even Waitrose looking rather ghostly. As for us, every day we simply used our food storage and our stored water from our pantry, and we used our fuel reserve (a couple of small cans) to go to work. We cycled everywhere and enjoyed the lack of heavy traffic.

What was the difference? Unlike perhaps the majority of people, we were prepared for everyday emergencies. We had stored a bit of food and water every time we did our shopping, and in the end we had almost a years supply of food, which we rotated regularly. Although we had a less than generous paycheque, we managed to put away enough to enjoy peace of mind first, and no stress later, during the crisis. Many other families had done the same, as they believed in the concept of preparing ahead for possible emergencies and for a rainy day.

The principle of self-reliance is to help ourselves first, so we can reach to others in need. Help cannot come from an empty shelf or purse. We can't help ourselves, or others, if we are not self-sufficient to start with. I grew up with this principle engrained in my parents' life. They always stored in their pantry plenty of apples, onions, potatoes, nuts and cheese. We had a chest freezer full of bread, vegetables and meat.

My mum canned tomato sauce every summer, and we used it during winter. And all this took place while both of my parents worked full time on very demanding jobs, for their Import-Export company. No unexpected guest was ever turned away:

there was always something to offer and when a one meter-high layer of snow blocked our city for four weeks, back in the 80s, we managed to eat regularly every day.

Do learn about self-reliance and try to apply it in your everyday life!

For the complete story of the fuel strike, and to anticipate what may happen in similar situations, see http://en.wikipedia.org/wiki/Fuel_protests_in_the_United_Kingd om

18
STORING AND ROTATING FOOD, WATER AND SUPPLIES

"Adversity has the effect of eliciting talents which, in prosperous circumstances, would have lain dormant." (Horace, "Satires")

Having food storage means putting away some food and water to use at a later time, before the expiry day arrives. This method allows us to have a reserve of food should lack of work or an emergency arise, and it protects us from inflation at the same time. The topic is very well covered in plenty of websites and books, and therefore I will only give you some small tips; I would like to encourage you to learn about it as soon as possible, so you can get started, too.

What should I store?

It is a good idea to store what you eat, so later you can eat what you stored without losing your appetite. So, if you like meat and veggies, and hate dairies, do store meat and veggies. However, it is better to separate mentally our meals in two areas: fresh foods for daily use and staple, bulk foods.

Every-day foods are found among fresh fruit and vegetables, bread, milk, takeaways, doughnuts, biscuits, sauces, condiments, and whatever people will eat as a habit and buy daily or weekly. These are a bit difficult to store, unless you have a good size chest freezer. Also, they need rotating quickly because they expire in max 2 years or less (fresh food in fact will only last for a week or less). Long-term foods instead include those which you can safely store for many years, and yet will not lose much of their nutritional power, taste and texture. For example, did you know that as recent studies have shown, staples such as white rice, pasta, wheat, cereals and legumes such as lentils and beans can be stored for up to 20 years and still retain their nutritional value? Not so bad, after all!

And - by the way - they are much cheaper than the first group of foods, especially if bought wholesale - in bulk. These foods are certainly to be considered for long-term supply. Small reserves of water, or a good water filter, are also a very good idea. By water filter I don't mean a Brita jug but a British Berkefeld filter, based on ceramic and silver to filter impurities; this type of filter eliminates 99% of bacteria and makes almost any type of water safe.

Why should I store food and some water?

Because to survive we all need food, water and shelter. If we lose our job or our health, for long or short periods of time, we'll be glad we have put away something to sustain us in times of need. Our economy is not recovering at all, despite those rosy predictions of a +0.01% increase given by mainstream news journalists. Losing your job when you have credit card debt and no savings, a mortgage and nothing valuable to sell to raise cash, means simply that you will go hungry over a short period of time - and if your mortgage repayments stop, you are at risk of losing your property and becoming homeless. Impossible?

Let's look at some figures. The Council of Mortgage lenders (CML) has warned that house repossessions are likely to rise again in 2012 from 40,000 to 45,000. As the end of the chapter is far from here I shall quote my sources below.

Source: http://www.bbc.co.uk/news/business-13620099
UK home repossessions have risen by 48% in 2008
Source: http://news.bbc.co.uk/1/hi/business/7548877.stm

Unless we are the owners of our property, with no debt, and a secure job, our financial future is not 100% guaranteed. Moreover, sometimes people experience unemployment because of long-term illnesses, death of a spouse, and other unexpected circumstances, which can bring them down to their knees. Changes of technologies, for example, can make our profession obsolete. Do you think it would be easy to find work in 2015 if you have trained for example in the 80s, as a computer programmer using Pascal programming? Lots of professions around today did not exist 10 years ago, while others are disappearing. Therefore, storing a little bit for a rainy day is not at all a bad idea. It's actually sounding quite appealing to more and more people.

I don't have money to store any food - how can I prepare?

This is a typical question I am asked all the time; however, the good news is that everybody can store a little bit. Even if you have absolutely no money saved, every day you can put away a spoonful of rice or pasta, or some beans in a jar.

Now, every time you buy or receive some food, freeze some or put away one can of food. If you receive a bag of pasta, store some away. If you arrive home with three cans of food, put away one. You will be surprised to see how much you have stored in a couple of months. The important thing is to get started soon.

Then, keep going and adding variety, so you have some proteins (meat, beans), some carbohydrates, some fruit, vegetables, nuts and seeds. Add also long-term foods such as whole grains, rice, and legumes.

Did you know, for example, that popping corn lasts for many years? One big thing that can really help is to learn about sprouting vegetables and grains. (You can look in the sprouting sections of this book). In fact, home sprouted grains are incredibly filling and cheap to buy, and they can keep you alive if anything else fails to materialise. A simple cup of whole wheat can be boiled and eaten or can be sprouted for 3 days before eating it. When sprouted it will be as filling as when boiled; however, it will have a high number of vitamins and

Omega 3, and it will be more digestible than cooked wheat. I warmly suggest you study sprouting and discover the benefits of keeping and sprouting seeds and grains. Take advantage of special offers in shops; when something is much cheaper than usual, buy a little more and store it away. It is a good idea to write the expiry date on your cans and packages of food before putting them on your shelves. If you keep a thick permanent black marker in your chosen food storage area, it will be automatic to scribble the date on the container. This will save you a lot of time later, when you are trying to work out what needs to be eaten and you end up spending hours looking for small print everywhere. Also, do try the products before you store lots of them. Once we bought some Asda economy mashed potatoes, and only a year later we found out that the taste was absolutely horrible and not worth buying that product ever again, let alone eating it with or without a crisis!

How do I use my food storage?

Another usual question. Unless you are storing Tiger worms, your food storage should be as appetising as your normal meals, and it can be used as normal. For example, storing fresh fruit for more than two years isn't possible, but it is easy to store canned or dehydrated fruit. A can of economy peaches costs around 38 pence at the moment and in two years it will expire - just before the expiry date, you can open it, mix it with fresh fruit and have a lovely fruit salad.

Dehydrated fruit can be eaten as it is (as a snack) or it can be placed in water to be re-hydrated, then mixed in a food processor, to obtain an instant fruit jam with an intense taste. Canned, dried or frozen veggies are excellent for pasta sauces, soups and casseroles.

Pasta, rice, couscous and whole grains can be a base to use a can of veggies, or can be eaten simply with some oil and whatever spices are available. Seeds are excellent on salads and very nutritious. If you learn now how to rotate your stored food, there won't be a sudden shock when your source of income disappears for a length of time. Of course, the best way to store food is to grow your own (see gardening section) so you can store the surplus, by canning, freezing or dehydrating. There are plenty of books, articles and websites on the topic with recipes to please even the most demanding palate.

What if my supplies go off?

Then you haven't been using and rotating your food storage regularly, or you have stored them at a temperature higher than 18°C or in full sunlight. When you buy food or drinks, *always* check the expiry date and then use a large, black permanent marker to write down month and year on top. For example May 2012 could be "05/12". Then, when you arrange your cans, bottles etc. keep them together arranging them by type and date. For example, sweetcorn cans in one area, tomato sauce in another etc. If you put the newest product on the back and the oldest in front, you will hardly ever forget to use it in time. And by the way, apart from egg pasta and canned meat, all the other types of canned food are completely edible well after the expiry date - up to 10-12 months after it. As I said previously, some foods are known to last 20+ years. White rice, pasta, popping corn and wheat/bulgur are some of them; therefore it makes sense to store them in bulk.

What about water?

Water is essential for washing, preparing food and drinking so I would suggest that you store a few bottles of water when possible and rotate them every year as they acquire a foul taste. If you forget to open and use up a bottle after the expiration date, and don't want to waste it, open the lid and shake the bottle for a while, until new oxygen has penetrated the water and given it a better taste. If it still tastes ugly you can always use it for washing or watering plants.

If you have funds I also suggest you research some portable home water filters. There are many around and my favourite is the British Berkefeld filter, which is used by many agencies to help Third World countries to have potable water and also as relief after disasters. It consists of a ceramic filter with silver particles, which finely filters any water, even from a puddle, and makes it perfectly clean and safe to drink, improving its taste tenfold. Water is essential for survival and can't be ignored in a good preparedness plan.

Otherwise you might want to research how Indians and primitive people, scouts etc. filter water by distillation and other methods so you can survive if all the water is gone or is polluted. Find a website explaining the principles of water filtering, print out the instructions and study them, then file them away in a special emergency folder: you never know when it will become useful.

I wouldn't count on Government, charities, agencies or churches to feed everybody should problems arise: have you heard of any of them storing food and supplies for you? If yes, please send me their contact details! And lastly: emergencies don't happen only abroad! The UK is not highly seismic, but we have experienced plenty of difficulties with fuel strikes, ice, snow, flooding, pollution and riots.

Other aspects of self-reliance and some suggestions:

- ✓ Invest in alternative energy and alternative ways of cooking.

- ✓ Grow your own food at home, in the garden or allotment.

- ✓ Sprout your own seeds and grains.

- ✓ Make your own compost.

- ✓ Prepare a 72-hour pack with dried foods, water and a sleeping bag, to keep you alive in case of emergency.

- ✓ Learn how to make and repair clothes and shoes.

- ✓ Learn knitting, spinning, weaving.

- ✓ Learn how to cook from scratch.

- ✓ Acquire and learn from books on how to make anything.

- ✓ Ask your friends to show you how to do something new.

- ✓ Buy hair-cutting equipment and learn how to use it.

- ✓ Grow your own herbs and spices to make tea and healing infusions

- ✓ Acquire and learn from DIY books and self-help books.

- ✓ Replace expensive meat with the cheaper chicken.

- ✓ Swap garden produce surplus and other goods (clothes included) with your friends.

- ✓ Share car trips when possible.

- ✓ Buy and use a bike and acquire a manual on how to keep it in order.

- ✓ Use your car as little as possible and shop around for cheaper running cars and cheaper insurance; reduce shopping trips and drive smoothly. Fill up with fuel in the morning, when there is less air in the dispenser.

- ✓ Recycle and eliminate clutter in your home.

- ✓ Learn soap making and candle making and use your skills to make fabulous gifts.

- ✓ Learn how to make your own washing up liquid, shampoo and moisturisers using everyday ingredients.

✓ Keep one or two spare can openers for your stored canned food.

✓ Care about others and offer your service. Help when ice and snow arrive. If you are physically able to, pick up your shovel, and clear up your own path all the way to your gates or front door, so you and your visitors can safely commute to and from your house. If everybody takes care of his own land and paths, companies included, everybody will enjoy safer paths when they venture outdoors.

✓ Expand your range of services. If you are able to, do ask your children or friends to help you and clear the path of your elderly or disabled neighbour so he can step outside safely. Bring a meal to somebody in need or help someone doing some work in the garden. Volunteer for charities and in hospitals and emergency departments. Serving others as a family is a brilliant way of building character in our offspring, and coincidentally, it helps to see our own problems under a new light. Not to mention how many pounds of unwanted weight you can shed by shoveling snow or digging a garden for an hour! Much cheaper than a gym workout!

✓ Re-write and update your C.V., adding specific details on how you can help a company to produce more, save money and solve problems. Employers are on the look for problem solvers, not for dusty skills and a laid-back attitude. If you still have a job, treasure the timeless words of Vince Lombardi: *"If you aren't fired with enthusiasm, you **will** be fired with enthusiasm."* Especially during difficult times!

✓ Give your best and earn a good reputation at work - your helpful attitude will pay its dividends when the boss will be choosing who to keep and who to send home.

✓ Clothing and fashion: adult clothes of good quality, made with durable fabric and in timeless, polished styles, can last for over 20 years. Not the same is true for cheap and cheerful outfits bought for a couple of pounds in supermarkets! Sometimes spending more means saving in the long run.

✓ Buy good quality shoes, which sustain the foot properly and have the correct height: wearing high heels often will cause spinal and neck problems in the long run, and damage to ankles and tendons. Wearing extremely flat shoes, with no arch support, will also bring pains when older, and the expenses for podiatrist, insoles, treatments etc. will be much greater than having used good shoes for all your life.

"Now, try to remember Dulcie, *where* is the can opener?"

19
NATURAL BEAUTY BEYOND BOTOX AND SURGERY

"A person who has good thoughts cannot ever be ugly. You can have a wonky nose and a crooked mouth and a double chin and stick-out teeth, but if you have good thoughts they will shine out of your face like sunbeams and you will always look lovely." (Roald Dahl)

Our nation spends £10.5 billion every year on grooming so I assume that everyone wishes to be clean and beautiful. In 2006, the New Woman Magazine published a report stating that every day a woman applies to her skin twelve cosmetic products, mounting up to 2 kilograms in a year, consisting of 175 different chemicals and spending on average £3,000. This amount adds up to a staggering £182,528 for an adult lifetime of beauty products and treatments. That's enough to buy a 3-bedroom house! And I haven't worked out how much we spend for shampoos, bath bubbles, shaving foams etc.

Our spending for cosmetics finds its main motivation in a search for cleanliness and maybe for an unachievable eternal youth and beauty, as pushed on us daily by magazines and media who think nothing of Photoshopping "imperfect", anorexic models to make them look impossibly perfect. Their looks are honestly unachievable but cosmetic companies claim otherwise and we want to believe them!

It's good to look attractive, neat, clean, and well groomed, but I wonder how essential it is to try to achieve perfection through the following products or procedures:

- ✓ anti-aging creams (some of which are just scams)

- ✓ Botox injections (to become even stiffer than Barbie)

- ✓ surgery to augment, shrink, cut off, tone up and remodel every part of our anatomy (they ought to add brain remodeling, too, but no Botox-filled show-girl seems to care about increasing her brain size)

- ✓ extreme diets, anorexia (it is perfectly possible to become skinny and still look unattractive)

- ✓ fake tan all year round (the highway to early wrinkles)

- ✓ hours spent straightening/curling hair (the easiest way to make your hair look lifeless by 45)

- ✓ acrylic decorated nails (impractical, and an excellent breeding ground for fungal infections)

- ✓ acid skin exfoliants (aggressive to our skin)

- ✓ denial of aging as a natural process (a mental attitude problem of our "modern" society)

We need to think of why we are spending so much on cosmetics because that, dear friends, doesn't just impact our emotional being but our bank accounts (as seen above) and our health (and now I will give you a few ideas).

How to achieve a natural beauty

"For beautiful eyes, look for the good in others; for beautiful lips, speak only words of kindness; and for poise, walk with the knowledge that you are never alone." (Audrey Hepburn)

I wouldn't mind being tall, beautiful and charming, but I am quite comfortable with myself now that I am approaching my middle age. My innate sense of humour does help, especially when I stare at my face in the morning! Eeek! Thankfully my eyesight isn't very good, either. So, let's see a few principles about how to become naturally beautiful. I found some good advice around - take it or leave it as you please!

The first principle is how confident we are in our looks. If we think we look beautiful, we will act beautiful. So, careful not to look for too long at those fake images that do not reflect achievable or real standards. Glossy fashion and beauty magazines, rather than inspiring us, often make us feel like low achievers. Absence of wrinkles doesn't automatically imply charming looks. George Clooney has plenty of wrinkles but they seem to improve his looks, correct? Why women are bullied to think otherwise when it comes to their skin?

The second principle must be to live in a healthy way: eat plenty of fresh, raw fruit and vegetables, exercise or dance, walk etc. regularly, get enough sleep every night and avoid junk food, drugs, smoke and alcohol. Those bad habits are to be avoided totally as, in the long term, they cause several health problems, ranging from obesity, skin blemishes and wrinkles, to weak nails and bad breath, gum diseases, stained teeth and so on.

Everything but glamorous huh? Third and last, use very few, basic and natural cosmetics to clean and tone hair and skin; massage your skin daily to improve circulation, instead of relying on creams to achieve a good flow of blood. Don't make your makeup look obvious, choose natural colours, avoiding looking like a clown. If nobody can recognise you unless you are wearing make-up, well, sorry, but something might be really wrong with your self-confidence!

How safe are our beauty products and our toiletries?

"Taking joy in living is a woman's best cosmetic."
(Rosalind Russell)

We are taught by constant media advertising that we need to be clean, perfumed, hygienic, pleasant and so on. It's wonderful to be clean and look beautiful, but at times we are using far too many products; the vast majority of them are actually toxic for our body and the problem is that toxins are absorbed easily through the largest organ of our body: our skin.

Starting with shampoo and shower gels, bubble baths, toothpaste and mouth wash, lipstick, make up products, nail polish, moisturisers and tanning creams, there are literally thousands of products available, filled with non regulated chemical substances some of which are either known allergens, or carcinogenic, or skin irritants, or all the above.

Have you ever come out of the shower/bath, and felt the urgency to scratch your skin? Does your skin look extremely dry and flaky after using soaps or gels? Do you need to apply a moisturiser after washing or your skin feels too tight and uncomfortable?

Then you could be among the millions whose skin is irritated by chemical detergents, containing mostly SLS or paraben (foaming agent and preservative). Before you fall from your chair, may I invite you to google "safety of cosmetics" or "paraben", "SLS" and other ingredients commonly used in cosmetic production. There are also plenty of books on the subject: I wonder why?

If you do a search on the internet, you will find out that many people are concerned about the safety of the chemicals contained in everyday toiletries and are looking for natural alternatives. Because every item we use brings into our body substances that will have a cumulative effect on our health.

I shall start by giving you a simple example: nail polish. It contains a handful of dangerous substances, especially those nail polishes which promise to make your nails stronger. One of the ingredients used in them is Formaldehyde, or Formaldehyde-based preservatives. (They are also contained in other products, hair care products, baby wipes etc.).

These preservatives release formaldehyde (which is known to be carcinogenic) and have been linked to cancer, developmental problems, endocrine disruption, allergies, immune system toxicity and more. Formaldehyde is also used to preserve corpses before burial and is present in cigarettes.

How nice to spread it on our nails! You don't need to despair if you give up nail polish. If you want to have strong nails, and you don't have a particular disease causing loss of minerals, you don't need one of those really expensive hardening nail polishes. All you need is to eat a generous bowl of mixed fresh greens every day, dressed with olive oil and some sesame seeds or mixed seeds, and within 10 days your nails will be much stronger than you have ever seen them before. Keep going for a month and you will be impressed with your perfect nails. Stop eating those salads.... and your nails will become soft and fragile again. Obviously the industry has no interest in selling lettuce for 50p, so they promote these ludicrously expensive products and we fall in their trap. If you don't believe me, try it yourself and let me know what results you are getting, by posting on my blog!

Another example of a universally spread chemicals is SLS - if you google it you will find over 600.000 results to learn from. Let's talk about it again. SLS (Sodium Lauryl Sulphate) is contained in the majority of shampoos and toothpastes, cosmetics, mouthwashes, hair colouring mixes and of course all house detergents. Why? Because Sodium Lauryl Sulphate is a very harsh detergent born as an industrial degreasant and garage floor cleaner. When applied to human skin, it has the effect of stripping off the oil layer and then irritating and eroding the skin, leaving it rough and pitted.

SLS has been shown in research to irritate skin, and be linked to cancer, disruption of the endocrine system, reproductive toxicity and neurotoxicity. Some people find they get canker sores when using SLS toothpastes. I have talked about SLS in the oral health section so I need say no more. There isn't much difference in washing our hair with SLS-based shampoos or using Jif - they both strip our hair of their natural defences, although shampoos definitely smell better. Aluminium is also widely used as a component of facial and skin products, sunscreens and deodorant, and in cosmetics; however, as it builds up in the brain it contributes to Alzheimer's and other brain disorders. Just imagine how good it will feel to lose your mind at age 65 and know that those "essential" toiletries have played a big part in it. Oh - but you won't remember it, because your memory will be gone!

I should stop here. Now look at your pile of chemically based beauty products and toiletries and ask yourself: are they really worth my health and expense? Could it be that one of the many causes of increased cancer and allergy levels in the industrial world is indeed the huge amount of chemicals we put on our skin?

Did you know that the above products are not regulated like foods and medicines, although they are absorbed through our skin? The industry can put whatever it wants inside a product, make a lovely package claiming perfect results and convince the masses that all is well.

My point for the purpose of this book is that we can greatly lower our expenses if we reduce the amount of unnecessary beauty and cleaning products, choose or make natural ones, and work from the inside out to create real beauty from within instead of disguising our sickness with a thick layer of chemicals.

Another personal consideration is that if we rely mostly on our youthful looks to create, and then keep our relationships alive, we are going to be at a disadvantage when time will inexorably leave its marks all over our bodies - whatever cosmetics we use. Then, when our partners will look elsewhere for those youthful looks that we have worshipped so intensively, it might be too late to build up our relationship on lasting values such as love, romance, honesty, caring, having fun together, etc.

At the end of the day there are plenty of stunning looking men and women who are not as happy as we think, and who are dealing with the same problems that we have as mortal people, from pain and sickness to divorce, loss of work, drugs and alcoholism. But - of course - this aspect of their life is pushed aside by the media when they are advertising eternal beauty and success - when we buy cosmetics are we chasing a fragile dream? It may be cheaper to eat fresher foods with good anti-oxidant properties. You don't need to buy a special yoghurt to have anti-oxidants.

The antioxidant values of foods listed are expressed in ORAC (Oxygen Radical Absorbance Capacity) units, a unit of measurement for antioxidants developed by the National Institute on Aging in the National Institutes of Health (NIH).

Here is a list of foods containing a good percentage of anti-oxidants, which as we know decrease skin aging naturally. Generally speaking, all nuts and dried fruits have really high levels of anti-oxidants.

- ✓ 9.5 - raw artichokes
- ✓ 7.6 - raw pistachio nuts
- ✓ 6.6 - apples
- ✓ 6.6 - dried garlic powder
- ✓ 3.8 - dates
- ✓ 3.1 - raw peanuts
- ✓ 1.8 - raw red grapes

Look up the website of the National Institute on Aging, for an explanation about ORAC: http://www.oracvalues.com

Regarding the safety of cosmetics you can try websites such as:
http://www.mysensitiveskincare.com
http://safecosmetics.org
http://www.cosmeticdatabase.com

Keira wondered why she didn't get any help when she popped out for some bread and milk.

20
HOW TO MAKE YOUR OWN BEAUTY PRODUCTS

"Beauty is not in the face; beauty is a light in the heart."
(Kahlil Gibran)

You might think that it's impossible, but making safer, wonderfully scented beauty products at home is not very difficult at all. There are several books available on the subject and several suppliers of natural ingredients. One good textbook for example is *The Holistic Beauty Book: With Over 100 Natural Recipes for Beautiful Skin*, author Star Kechara, £7.92 in Amazon.co.uk. This book contains recipes for products to be used on your skin, including lipstick and bath products. A longer search might find many more books - or you can try your local library and some blogs on the subject.

I shall propose a few combinations to try out, before you commit to buy specialised books. Although you will find that, for professional results, you might have to become acquainted with new things such as beeswax, coconut oil etc., once you have learned the basic principles, you will be able to design your own recipes for most beauty products.

I have listed some here just to show you how easy it is to make your own cosmetics. I gathered them from all over the place over the years. Some are unisex and some not; they can be used for babies and adults alike. Others are designed to help soothing pain and discomfort. For proper, detailed instructions on a full range of products refer to books, websites, etc. The recipes below do not contain any preservatives and therefore are not going to last more than 3-5 days for recipes containing liquids and 1 month for the dry recipes. So, choose the most appealing product and look for ingredients! Have fun, try to achieve a good result and compliment yourself for taking charge of your own beauty routine. You might not become a stunning beauty overnight but your body will be thankful for your good choice of ingredients.

Quick & Easy Lip Balm

Ingredients:

- ✓ 1 tsp. beeswax
- ✓ 2 tsp. coconut oil
- ✓ 1 vitamin E capsule
- ✓ 2-3 drops essential oil (mint, strawberry, orange etc.)

Instructions:

Melt beeswax, coconut, and vitamin E together. Then add your favourite essential oil. Place in a tube or pot. Note: a way to melt the ingredients is to use a double boiler.

Baby ointment for nappy rash

Ingredients:

- ✓ 16 oz. (450g) Sweet Almond Oil
- ✓ 8 oz. (225g) Shea Butter
- ✓ 8 oz. (225g) Jojoba Oil
- ✓ 4½ oz. (125g) Virgin Coconut Oil
- ✓ 4½ oz. (125g) Beeswax
- ✓ 2 Drops Calendula Absolute
- ✓ Essential oils: chamomile, lavender and tea tree

Instructions:

Mix the oils, the butter and the beeswax in a double boiler until the wax and the butter are melted. Now stir 2 drop of Calendula and mix. Add essential oils (1 drop each) and then pour into jars.

Powdered blush

Ingredients:

- ✓ 1 tsp. (5ml) Arrowroot Powder or cornstarch
- ✓ 1 tsp. (5ml) Pearlescent Mica Powder (for hue and intensity reduce or increase amounts)
- ✓ 1 tsp. (5ml) White Kaolin Clay
- ✓ ½ tsp. (2.5ml) Magnesium Sulphate
- ✓ jojoba oil (as needed).

Instructions

Add all powdered ingredients to a small clean bowl and mix thoroughly. Use a spoon to pour them in a wide mouth jar. If the blush doesn't quite stay on your (possibly dry) skin, try to add a few drops of jojoba oil.

Quick & easy hand cream

Ingredients:

- ✓ 1 tbsp. (15ml) honey
- ✓ 2 tbsp. (30ml) avocado oil
- ✓ 2 tbsp. (30ml) glycerin
- ✓ 1½ cups (350ml) finely ground almonds

Instructions

Mix the avocado oil, honey, and glycerin in a bowl, and then stir in a sufficient amount of almonds to form a paste. Apply to hands and rub in well until it soaks into the skin and the almond remains fall off. The cream produced will be sufficient for several applications.

Yogurt & Banana Face mask

Ingredients:

- ✓ 1 tsp. (5ml) plain yoghurt
- ✓ ¼ ripe banana
- ✓ ¼ tsp. (1.5ml) of Vitamin E 1000 IU

Instructions

Mash the ingredients in a bowl to achieve a smooth mixture. Then apply to your skin and leave for 10 minutes or until dry, before washing off with lukewarm water. Your skin will be smoother and softer.

Clay face mask

Ingredients:

- ✓ clay (choose the right type for your skin type)
- ✓ water or other wetting agent (milk, honey, floral water)
- ✓ jojoba essential oil

Instructions

Mix the ingredients to form a paste and apply it to your skin; leave it to dry for 15 minutes, then rinse well and dry. This is a good mask to purify greasy skin!

After Shave lotion

Ingredients

- ✓ 11 oz. (310g) distilled water
- ✓ ½ oz. (15g) Rice Bran Oil
- ✓ ½ oz. (15g) Borage Oil
- ✓ ½ oz. (15g) Hempseed Oil
- ✓ 1½ oz. (45g) Mango Butter
- ✓ 1½ oz. (45g) Emulsifying Wax
- ✓ ½ oz. (15g) Wheatgerm Oil

Instructions:

Using a double boiler, heat up the above ingredients until they reach about 160°F (70°C), mixing well. Turn off the gas and allow to cool to room temperature. Mix in a blender until you obtain a thick and soothing lotion.

Honey and almond facial scrub

Ingredients:

- ✓ 1 tsp. (5ml) ground almonds
- ✓ 1 tsp. (5ml) colloidal oatmeal (coarse)
- ✓ 1 tsp. (5ml) honey
- ✓ 1 tsp. (5ml) buttermilk powder
- ✓ Water

Instructions:

In a bowl, mix the ingredients to achieve a thick paste adding as much water as needed to achieve the result, then use as a normal face scrub. Note: good natural exfoliants are: salts, sugars, fruit seeds, fruit fibres, nut meals, ground loofah, ground pumice and grain powders.

Basic scented soap recipe (cold process)

(I am not talking about hot processed soap here, as high temperatures are reached during the preparations, and therefore it needs more care and detailed instructions than I can give you in my book)

Ingredients

- ✓ 1 bar of neutral white soap, not perfumed, non allergenic

- ✓ 9 oz. (250ml) boiling water in double boiler or Pyrex glass container

- ✓ 2 tsp. (10ml) of your favourite herb (chamomile, lavender, citrus...)

- ✓ 6 drops of your favourite essential oil matching the above herb (mint, citrus etc.) Avoid using more than 2 fragrances or the soap won't have a defined scent anymore.

- ✓ 3 drops of food colourant (optional)

- ✓ biscuit cutters or chocolate moulds (optional)

Instructions:

Grate the soap and slowly pour on it the hot water, stirring until it melts. When the mixture reaches a jelly consistency add the other ingredients. Mix well with a metal spoon and choose either option: pour liquid soap into moulds or leave to solidify for a little while. When the temperature is comfortable, form some small balls with your hands or pat into biscuit cutters until desired shape is achieved. Leave the new soaps to dry for 24 hours and then to cure for 4 weeks. You can also wrap them with tissue paper and use as a gift!

Soothing cream (excellent for eczema)

Ingredients:

- ✓ 4 oz. (110g) jojoba oil
- ✓ 20 drops evening primrose oil
- ✓ 12 drops lavender essential oil
- ✓ 12 drops roman chamomile essential oil

Instructions

Use a bowl to mix all the ingredients and apply at the first sign of red, patchy skin.

Skin toner

Ingredients:

- ✓ 1 cup (240ml) aloe vera gel
- ✓ 2 tbsp. (30ml) chamomile tea
- ✓ 2 tbsp. (30ml) vitamin E oil
- ✓ 5 drops peppermint essential oil

Instructions:

Mix together the aloe vera gel and chamomile tea, and then heat slowly in a double boiler. Allow the mixture to cool and strain off any solids using a tea strainer. Now add the vitamin E and peppermint oils, stir a bit more until smooth. Pour into a bottle. Makes approx. 9 oz. (250g). This is very soothing and refreshing especially after being exposed to the sun.

Mint Toothpaste

Ingredients:

- ✓ 2 tsp. (10ml) baking soda
- ✓ 4 tsp. (20ml) arrowroot powder
- ✓ ¼ tsp. (1.5ml) sea salt
- ✓ 4 tsp. (20ml) glycerin
- ✓ 10-15 drops of peppermint or other essential oil.

Instructions:

Mix well in a bowl and pour into a glass jar; use as a normal toothpaste.

Nail anti-fungal oil

Ingredients:

- ✓ 2 tsp. (10ml) sweet almond essential oil
- ✓ 1 tsp. (5ml) hempseed essential oil
- ✓ 10 drops vitamin E oil
- ✓ 10 drops tea tree essential oil
- ✓ 3 drops myrrh essential oil
- ✓ 5 drops lavender essential oil

Instructions:

In a bowl mix all the ingredients and then pour in a dark glass container. Apply to the nails every day.

Soothing Joint Ointment (to relieve joint pains)

Ingredients:

- ✓ 2/3 cup (160ml) avocado butter
- ✓ 1 tbsp. (15ml) menthol crystals
- ✓ 1 cup (240ml) sesame seed oil
- ✓ 10 drops of eucalyptus essential oil
- ✓ 3 drops of lemon essential oil

Instructions:

Mix the sesame seed oil and menthol crystals using a double boiler and heat the mixture until the crystals melt. Now remove from the heat and add avocado butter and essential oils. Stir and pour into jars.

Shoe Powder

Ingredients:

- ✓ 1/4 cup (60ml) Baking Soda
- ✓ 1/8 cup (30ml) Arrowroot Powder
- ✓ 1 tbsp. (15ml) Dendritic salt (it has an unusually high capacity to absorb moisture before becoming wet)
- ✓ 3 tbsp. (45ml) fragrance (Baby talcum is good)

Instructions:

Mix in a bowl your chosen fragrance with the dendritic salt. Add baking soda and arrowroot powder. Now you can sprinkle in shoes/sneakers for fresh feet all day long.

Color Restorer shampoo for Grey Hair

Ingredients

- ✓ ½ cup (120ml) dried sage
- ✓ ¼ cup (60ml) dried rosemary

Instructions

Simmer rosemary and sage in 2 cups of water for 30 minutes, and then steep for several hours. Apply to gray hair and allow to dry, then shampoo. Repeat weekly until desired shade is reached, then once a month for maintenance.

Natural Hairspray

Ingredients:

- ✓ ½ orange
- ✓ ½ lemon

Instructions

Chop fruit into small pieces and place in a pot with 2 cups water. Boil until reduced by half. Cool, strain, and place in a spray bottle. Store in the refrigerator or add one oz. rubbing alcohol to store at room temperature for up to two weeks. Add more water to reduce stickiness, if desired.

Clarifying Cider Vinegar Rinse

Ingredients:

- ✓ ½ cup (120ml) cider vinegar
- ✓ 1½ cups (360ml) very cold water

Instructions:

Mix ingredients in a plastic bottle. Shampoo and rinse hair, as usual. Pour vinegar rinse through hair, do not rinse again. Ratio of vinegar to water may be adjusted according to the amount of clarifying needed or frequency of use. This rinse will effectively remove product build-up from hair including silicone and leave it very soft and shiny, without any smell of vinegar.

Raspberry & Vanilla Bubble Bath

Ingredients:

- ✓ 8 oz. (225g) neutral liquid soap (with no fragrance)
- ✓ 2 oz. (55g) distilled water8 drops vanilla essential oil
- ✓ 6 drops raspberry essential oil
- ✓ 2 drops red food coloring (optional)

Instructions:

Mix all and pour into a container.

An excellent website to check out is www.aromantic.co.uk Also, try http://www.phytobotanica.com (UK grown and distilled essential oils and flower waters)

21
BASIC HERBAL REMEDIES FOR COMMON AILMENTS

"Natural Healing with Herbs for a Healthier You"
(Dr. Christopher)

As any Herbalist will tell you, there are many problems that can be eased or solved by eating wholesome foods and using the right herbs. I will list some simple ways of getting rid of basic problems. My suggestions are here just to get you started and have not been evaluated by any F.D.A. type organisation. Generally speaking, whatever problem we encounter, apart of emergency situations (broken bones, heart attack etc.) we can start with a system cleanse/detox - as soon as the bowels are clean, things magically improve! It is sensible to be followed by a qualified Herbalist in order to do the right cleanse without jeopardising our health.

Celery juice as a painkiller

If you are suffering from pains - especially arthritis - do your research on the web about the fantastic properties of celery. This plant has been proven in proper medical studies to lower chronic pain from 60% to 100% within weeks. Celery is a diuretic and therefore should not be over used if a serious kidney problem is present. Celery can be taken fresh, as a juice or in tablets.

Raspberry leaves, vitamin C and Echinacea for colds

Whenever a cold starts up in my family, we immediately take three things three times a day and it works for us:

13 drops of Echinacea tincture mixed with honey. Or, as it is alcoholic, we put the Echinacea in boiling water and wait a bit

until the alcohol has evaporated. Echinacea is available in all the supermarkets and health food/herbal stores/websites.

1 tablet of Vitamin C slow release

1 raspberry leaf tea mixed with honey

Echinacea boosts the immune system extremely quickly so that the body sends help to the infected area immediately. Vitamin C also fights the infection. Raspberry tea leaves are excellent as expectorants.

Usually, if we take the above products at the first onset of a cold, within 24 hours we are free of symptoms. We then continue the therapy for 2-3 days just in case. At the same time, if a cold begins, it is better to restrict meals to fresh fruit and vegetables, cut sugar completely (as it slows down the immune system) and of course eliminate dairies (congestion, difficulty breathing, allergies and hay fever are scientifically proven to be well connected with dairy consumption, and when people have a cold things get even worse). Please note that if you suffer from Lupus (an auto-immune disease) you should avoid Echinacea.

Tooth abscess

Dr. Christopher taught that an abscess contains lots of toxins that the body hasn't been able to get rid of through the normal process of elimination. When my son developed a huge abscess on the gum just over a wobbly milk tooth, our dentist prescribed him the customary antibiotic and asked him to return in two days.

Little did she know that 4 cloves of garlic are in fact, equivalent to an adult dose of penicillin. So the Family Herbalist in charge (myself) prescribed to my son to chew 3 cloves of garlic that day and to drink Echinacea and Zinc.

Needless to say, within 24 hours the abscess was completely gone, to the astonishment of our dentist. Avoid over-riding your system with antibiotics if you can: garlic is the most powerful antiviral plant you can find right in your kitchen. We might as well use garlic when possible!

To learn more about holistic health, I invite you to read what my mentors and teachers have to say and form your own opinion about this subject.

Dr. Christopher: http://www.herballegacy.com
Dr. Shultze: http://www.herbdoc.com

22
TAKING CARE OF YOUR MIND AND SPIRIT

"Love and kindness are the very basis of society. If we lose these feelings, society will face tremendous difficulties; the survival of humanity will be endangered" (Dalai Lama)

Having a positive attitude about life's challenges, feeling peaceful and calm, can be especially useful during recession times. The constant fear of losing one's job or becoming ill can be lessened with thoughtful preparation for the future. There is so much that one can do to improve his situation and give a positive contribution to society. Look at your attitude towards your challenges and start looking at them as opportunities to grow and learn.

I am gathering here some of my favourite quotes about the subject.

- ✓ Offer service in your family or community: there is always somebody who is faring much worse than you. This helps to keep things in perspective, to feel more content and to write something that looks great on any C.V. Service can also inspire you to change direction in your life, follow a new vocation or faith, enrich daily life and inspire others.

- ✓ Look for opportunities to serve in periods other than Christmas: people have needs all year round, not just in December! You may find that losing yourself in serving others is an excellent remedy for depression and boredom, two big maladies of today's wealthy and somehow superficial society.

- ✓ Be honest and trustworthy in your dealings with others. Don't take home items from the office or school - one day your clear conscience might make the difference and you might get some unexpected help from somebody who has admired your honesty and integrity.

✓ Get involved with a musical club or group, a choir or something musical or artistic. Dancing, singing, being musical or artistic refines the spirit and creates positive emotions. Good, uplifting music helps to lift you up in difficult moments.

✓ If music is not your favourite subject, try learning about nature through gardening, horticulture, taking nature walks and appreciation of the beauty of the Earth.

✓ Read good books, learn new skills, keep your mind alert, listen to the news every day but believe only 50% of what you hear, try to work out what's going to happen next so you can be prepared should something serious happens.

✓ Spend quantity and quality time with your loved ones; having fun doesn't necessarily have to imply spending money. A relaxed chat with your wife can make her happy; joining in some entertainment with your husband will make him feel good. Kids need to do things with their parents rather than be given "stuff" by them.

✓ Teach your children to be thoughtful and to care for others, to develop self-reliance skills and to help in the home and in the garden. Catch them doing something good so you can praise them every day and create a positive environment in your home. As David McKay said, *"No success can compensate a failure in the home"*.

✓ Enjoy the little you already have, instead of always wishing for something more. Ken S. Keyes, Jr. wrote *"To be upset over what you don't have is to waste what you do have"* (Handbook to Higher Consciousness). To an extent, we can be happy with very little.

✓ Spend some time pondering what is important to you, what do you wish to achieve in the next year and how, and then brainstorm a plan about how you and maybe your family will work to achieve that aim. A goal not written down is merely a wish. If you don't have a goal, you are on the road to nowhere and you will feel the recession as a stumbling block.

✓ Refocus yourself and your priorities and don't freeze in fear at the thought of unemployment or recession but always remember that the best things in life are free.

✓ Thousands of people before us have survived serious recessions without mobile phones, computer games, government benefits, supermarkets, cars, and - would you believe it - they even managed to keep friends without Facebook and instant messaging! They could do it, and we can do it, too.

✓ And finally, stop moaning about your problems all day long and smile at life. As Jeffrey Holland famously put it in 2007, *"No misfortune is so bad that whining about it won't make it worse!"*

CONCLUSION

"A truly good book teaches me better than to read it. I must soon lay it down, and commence living on its hint... What I began by reading, I must finish by acting." (Henry David Thoreau)

Dear readers, it's been a pleasure to share with you some ideas on self-reliance and I am relieved that I got it all off my chest now. Well, almost all. In fact, I would love to continue our conversation with my blog and future talks on "how to" so we can grow together. That's why I have set up a blog where we can share ideas about coping with the recession. I hope that my imperfect English and the basic layout of this book haven't hindered your enjoyment too much. While I am no authority nor a professional in any of the areas I discussed, I do hope that you will find something in my book that will inspire you to research more, be prepared, be focused, and to get started in your personal journey to become as independent, industrious, creative and positive as possible. I haven't covered every single problem we may face, but only those situations where I was personally able to see good results and I can now recommend certain solutions that have worked for me.

Be optimistic, do your best and keep learning new things, preparing for what's coming and helping others along the way. As Thomas Monson said, *"The future is as bright as your faith"*.

Thanks for reading!

Franz Sidney

LINKS OF INTEREST

Please refer to my blog to click directly on any links and add your views! - http://backtobasicshub.blogspot.com

Meridian Magazine - http://www.ldsmag.com

Advice on employment, home storage, gardening, finances, and emergencies - http://www.providentliving.org

Dr. Christopher's teachings, herbal remedies by topic - http://www.herballegacy.com

Stunning, mostly raw food recipes and photos by Susan Powers http://www.rawmazing.com

Dairy consumption and health - http://vegetarian.org.uk/campaigns/whitelies/wlreport07.shtml

Excessive Calcium Causes Osteoporosis - http://www.4.waisays.com/ExcessiveCalcium.htm

Why Milk Won't Prevent Osteoporosis - https://www.msu.edu/~corcora5/food/vegan/osteo.html

Lots of scientific studies showing for example an increase of hip fractures in dairy eaters as compared to non-dairy eaters, and much more. Enough to make you think twice about that glass of milk! - http://www.thebabybond.com/MilkingYourBones.html

A cure for cavities. Excellent tips on how to heal cavities, with photos and explanations about which bacteria cause cavities, foods to avoid and so on - http://www.xenophilia.com/zb0017.htm

Scientific studies about washing dishes, with instructions and facts:
http://www.ncbi.nlm.nih.gov/pmc/articles/PMC1555674
http://answers.google.com/answers/threadview/id/248104.html
http://www.nursinginpractice.com/article/295/Washing_those_dirty_d ishes_in_public_and_in_private)
http://www.wikihow.com/Wash-Dishes
http://www.bbc.co.uk/dna/h2g2/A337006

USEFUL BOOKS

John Seymour (The Father of Self-Sufficiency) has written much on how to establish a self-reliant home. My favourite book from this author is *"The new complete book of self-sufficiency"*, Dorling Kindersley 2003, ISBN-13: 978 0 7513 6442 2.

"The entitlement trap - How to Rescue Your Child with a New Family System of Choosing, Earning, and Ownership" by Richard Eyre. This is a good guide if you want to learn how to instill children with a sense of ownership, responsibility, and self-sufficiency.

Reader's Digest *"Natural remedies"* - Health and healing the natural way. This book, reprinted in 1996, contains some very useful explanations on how to deal with common ailments using herbal remedies, manipulation and Chinese medicine. ISBN 0 276 42195 7.

"Fit for life" by Harvey and Marilyn Diamond. This book, published in 1985 by Bantam Books, is only available in UK charity shops and on the internet (EBay, Amazon). It explains all the myths about diets, who is behind the big dairy and alcohol industry, the benefits of whole grains and raw food, and offers tons of tasty recipes for weight- loss and energy. A must read, written by medical doctors and still enjoyable after many years. ISBN 0-553-17355-3

ABOUT THE AUTHOR

Franz Sidney was born in Italy in the last century and has lived in Italy, Greece, the U.S.A. and now the UK. She is married to a brilliant British organist and pipe organ builder. They have two children who fill their days with new discoveries and endless tasks. Franz holds qualifications in Fashion Design, Graphic Design, Language teaching, Family herbalism and British Sign Language. She has illustrated greeting cards, a Preparation Manual and a B.S.L. booklet. Franz is also a correspondent for the Meridian Magazine and runs several blogs on preparation, raw food, nutrition and herbal medicine.

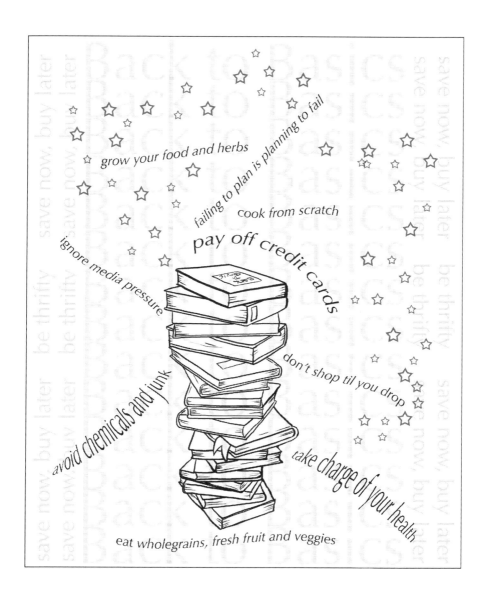

grow your food and herbs

failing to plan is planning to fail

cook from scratch

pay off credit cards

ignore media pressure

don't shop til you drop

avoid chemicals and junk

take charge of your health

eat wholegrains, fresh fruit and veggies

Made in the USA
San Bernardino, CA
11 December 2012